The Russian Revolution

An Enthralling Guide to a Major Event in the History of Russia

© Copyright 2023 - All rights reserved.

The content contained within this book may not be reproduced, duplicated, or transmitted without direct written permission from the author or the publisher.

Under no circumstances will any blame or legal responsibility be held against the publisher, or author, for any damages, reparation, or monetary loss due to the information contained within this book, either directly or indirectly.

Legal Notice:

This book is copyright protected. It is only for personal use. You cannot amend, distribute, sell, use, quote, or paraphrase any part, or the content within this book, without the consent of the author or publisher.

Disclaimer Notice:

Please note the information contained within this document is for educational and entertainment purposes only. All effort has been executed to present accurate, up-to-date, reliable, and complete information. No warranties of any kind are declared or implied. Readers acknowledge that the author is not engaging in the rendering of legal, financial, medical, or professional advice. The content within this book has been derived from various sources. Please consult a licensed professional before attempting any techniques outlined in this book.

By reading this document, the reader agrees that under no circumstances is the author responsible for any losses, direct or indirect, that are incurred as a result of the use of the information contained within this document, including, but not limited to, errors, omissions, or inaccuracies.

Free limited time bonus

Stop for a moment. We have a free bonus set up for you. The problem is this: we forget 90% of everything that we read after 7 days. Crazy fact, right? Here's the solution: we've created a printable, 1-page pdf summary for this book that you're reading now. All you have to do to get your free pdf summary is to go to the following website:

https://livetolearn.lpages.co/enthrallinghistory/

Once you do, it will be intuitive. Enjoy, and thank you!

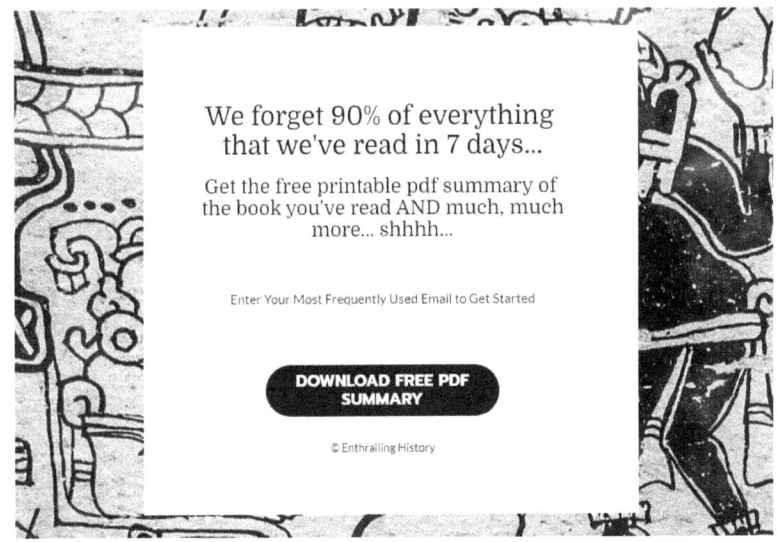

Table of Contents

INTRODUCTION 1
CHAPTER 1: SEEDS OF REVOLUTION: RUSSIA BEFORE THE STORM 4
CHAPTER 2: THE LAST TSAR: NICHOLAS II 14
CHAPTER 3: THE FEBRUARY REVOLUTION OF 1917 27
CHAPTER 4: DUAL POWER: THE PROVISIONALS AND THE PETROGRAD SOVIET 33
CHAPTER 5: THE OCTOBER REVOLUTION OF 1917 38
CHAPTER 6: THE RED TERROR 48
CHAPTER 7: CIVIL WAR AND THE STRUGGLE FOR CONTROL 60
CHAPTER 8: A "NEW ECONOMIC POLICY" – RUSSIA AFTER THE REVOLUTION 75
CHAPTER 9: STALINISM: THE REAL LEGACY OF THE RUSSIAN REVOLUTION 80
CHAPTER 10: KEY FIGURES OF THE RUSSIAN REVOLUTION 94
CONCLUSION 101
HERE'S ANOTHER BOOK BY ENTHRALLING HISTORY THAT YOU MIGHT LIKE 103
FREE LIMITED TIME BONUS 104
BIBLIOGRAPHY 105

Introduction

Amidst the chaos of the Great War and against the backdrop of decades of anti-tsarist actions in Russia, history gave birth to one of the most ambitious yet tragic endeavors in the history of mankind: the Russian Revolution. Finally, Marx's revolutionary ideas were put into action. The great chaos, bloodshed, and total abolishment of law and order, precursors of the Communist utopia according to Marx, swept across Russia like the Four Horsemen of the Apocalypse.

But Communist ideology was just one factor that brought about this great event. The man who would become the leader of the October Revolution, Vladimir Ilich Ulyanov, nicknamed Lenin, wasn't even in the country when the whole thing started. He was far away, in Switzerland, probably deeply shaken by all the previous failures at instigating the revolution. Amazed at the great turmoil finally taking over Russia, he rushed back via a legendary "sealed" train to Saint Petersburg, or as Russians call it, Petrograd.

Russia was considered an unlikely state to be the cradle of the first successful Communist revolution. Marx's ideas, it was believed, must first be realized in the most developed countries of Western Europe, much as Communism was considered the most progressive ideology of all by its proponents. Karl Marx himself had a peculiar disdain for Slavic peoples, and Russia was a country with one foot in the Medieval Ages. It had a very large peasant population and a small number of industry workers, the latter designated by the great Communist prophet as the carriers of the revolution. Peasants were only a hurdle.

While this small contradiction wasn't enough to stop the Russian Revolution, it prepared the scene for Russia's exceedingly violent and bloody submission to Communism.

In this book, we'll wrestle with the abundance of precursors to the Russian Revolution, such as anarchist movements in 19th-century Russia, the Russo-Japanese War, the Great War, and finally, the anachronistic Russian monarchy. We'll also cast light on the less-known characters of the great revolutionary saga—people like Bakunin, the chief philosopher of the anarchist movement, Sergey Nechayev, a prototypical Russian anarchist perfectly captured by the eye of Fyodor Dostoevsky, Pyotr Tkachev, the ideological father of the terrorist group that assassinated tsar Alexander II, and many others. But we'll also meet the usual suspects, such as Lenin and Stalin, with the goal of showcasing them for what they were.

Much like the French Revolution, the Russian Revolution(s) shook the world. Suddenly, this peculiar Goliath of a country rose from the ashes of a medieval empire. And while in the people of the USSR continuously experienced the dark side of Communism, the USSR served as an example of what workers can do. Spurred by the energy of Trotsky's "permanent revolution," people all around the world hoped that one day revolution would come to their countries, too. Ironically, while people in the USSR suffered under the burden of the new, often whimsical, and almost always cruel government, workers in the Western world saw significant improvements because major stakeholders were growing increasingly scared of having a Communist revolution in their own countries. At least briefly, an idealized vision of the USSR and Communism circulated around the world. Beneath the surface of this ideal lurked the dark reality: millions of dead people, destroyed countryside, endless purges, political strife, famine, disease, you name it. In this book, we'll tackle both sides of the story: the ideals (carried initially by fervently devoted youth), the chaos of the revolution, and the subsequent perversion of Communist ideals into their opposite.

It was once said that the dissolution of the USSR in 1989 was the "greatest geopolitical tragedy of the 20th century." If that's the case, the Russian Revolution constitutes some of the greatest tragedies in the history of mankind. But there's the other side: enthusiastic to the point of ecstasy, overly ambitious, proud, energetic, and worthy of eternal remembrance. These two aspects found ways to merge in increasingly complex ways, not only in grand events like the February or October

Revolutions but on a much more granular level. Lenin and Kerensky, two revolutionary leaders who quickly found themselves on opposite sides, sat in the same classroom as kids. People say that everything went haywire from the moment Lenin took over and Kerensky lost the upper hand. But Lenin had his good and bad sides. So did Trotsky, Stalin, and many others. As you'll see in this book, the granularity of the almost unfathomable merging of good and bad goes even further. There's no better scene for this than the Russian Revolution, which drew the best and the worst from people.

And then there's the repetition of history, historical irony, and rhyme. The most important political leaders of the French Revolution, as if by a rule, all encountered their final moments on the guillotine. It didn't take long for the Russian Revolution to devour its own children. One by one, they fell victim to internal striving for power, chiefly under the steel-cold Stalin. The man himself lived a miserable life, his family decimated by the devilish grin of the Red Terror. The seeds of this evil were sown much earlier, together with the seeds of good. Let's dig deep and uncover the earliest roots of the Russian Revolution, setting the scene for the grand event.

Chapter 1: Seeds of Revolution: Russia Before the Storm

Russian Empire

The revolutionaries had to fight against something, and this was, of course, the Russian Empire. We cannot understand the revolution in Russia without understanding the problems inherent to virtually all empires, the Russian Empire included. The early days of the Russian monarchy are steeped in legendary myths, with possible connections between early Russian dynasties and Nordic Viking invaders who went by the name of Rus'.[1] Although the Nordic roots of early Russia are barely discernible, the name stuck. One thing's certain: from the beginning (i.e., the late Migration Period around the 7th century CE), the population was predominantly Slavic, inhabiting, roughly speaking, the area of today's European Russia.

The first Russian dynasty, the Rurikids, carries the name of the legendary Nordic king, Rurik, who is attributed with forming the first state in European Russia. It is possible that, initially, Slavic and other tribes in this area were ruled by the less numerous but more powerful Nordic elite. But eventually, the Slavic elites took over, which we can infer from the names of the first (still legendary) rulers: Rurik, Oleg,

---

[1] PERRIE, Maureen; LIEVEN, Dominic CB; SUNY, Ronald Grigor (ed.). *The Cambridge History of Russia: Volume 1, From Early Rus' to 1689.* Cambridge University Press, 2006.

Askold, Dir, Oleg again, Igor, Olga, and Sviatoslav. From Sviatoslav onward, we only encounter Slavic names. This can be taken as evidence that the Rurikids (or Rurikovitch, as Russians might say) were influenced by the Slavic peoples that surrounded them, slowly learning their customs, tradition, and religion.

Religion, as we'll see, was also instrumental in the downfall of the Russian Empire. The early Rurikids were most likely pagans (of what kind, it's hard to say). It's likely that, after some time, they accepted the belief system of the East Slavs. Sviatoslav, who lived in the then-capital city of Kiev in the 10th century CE, was a pagan, as were his subordinates. His successor, Vladimir the Great, is credited with Christianizing Kievan Rus'.[2] The stories around this event are so entertaining that they ought to be briefly mentioned.

From the get-go, Vladimir favored Greek culture. It's no coincidence that soon after the decision to accept the Greek faith (around 987 or 988 CE), Vladimir married the daughter of the Byzantine Emperor Romanos II, Anna.[3] However, the choice to convert wasn't haphazardly made. Vladimir consulted his boyars (feudal lords) about what to do, and they advised him to first inquire about the customs and traditions of each religion. So, emissaries were sent, and returning to their ruler, they spoke of the illustrious service to God they witnessed in Tsarigrad (Constantinople). Islam, as practiced by the Bulgars, and the Germanic version of Christianity weren't as amazing and enchanting as Greek Christianity. Even before this, Vladimir understood that Islam wouldn't thrive among Russians: "But circumcision and abstinence from pork and wine were disagreeable to him. 'Drinking,' said he, 'is the joy of the Russes. We cannot exist without that pleasure.'"[4]

---

[2] KORPELA, Jukka. *Prince, Saint, and Apostle: Prince Vladimir Svjatoslavič of Kiev, His Posthumous Life, and the Religious Legitimization of the Russian Great Power*. Otto Harrassowitz Verlag, 2001.

[3] NESTOR, *Laurentian Text*. p. 112 Available at: https://www.mgh-bibliothek.de/dokumente/a/a011458.pdf

[4] Ibid. p. 97

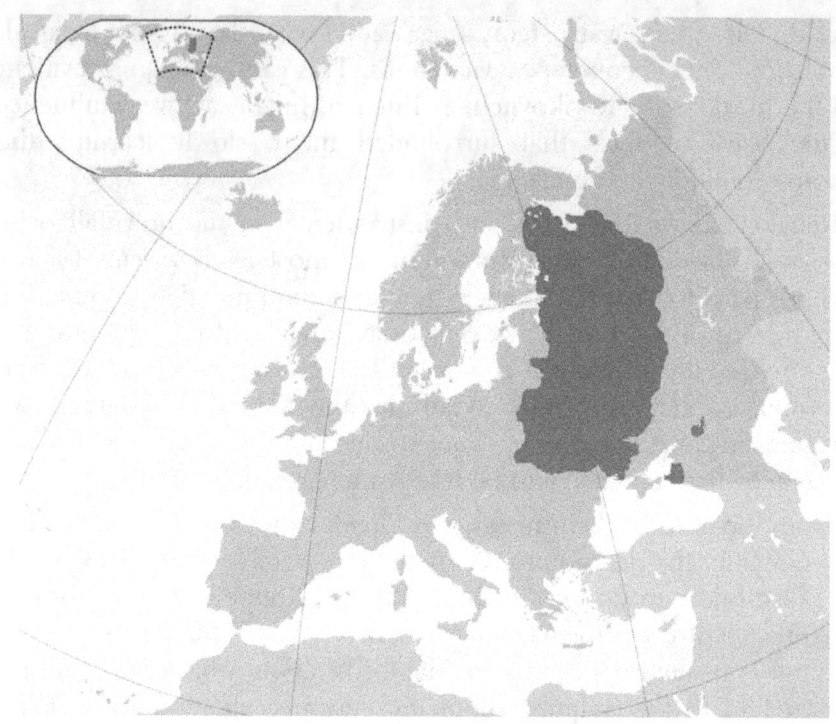

The extent of Kievan Rus' in the 11th century.
By Vitaliyf261 - Own work. Compare: Plokhy, Serhii (2006) The Origins of the Slavic Nations: Premodern Identities in Russia, Ukraine, and Belarus, Category: New York: Cambridge University Press, p. xiv ISBN: 978-0-521-86403-9., CC BY-SA 4.0, https://commons.wikimedia.org/w/index.php?curid=93773078

It is incredibly amusing to discover such a quote from the earliest days of the Russian state and even more amusing to see how the pleasure of alcohol might have shaped such an important decision as the adoption of this or that religion. As we'll soon see, alcohol played an important part in Russian history, revolutions included.

Slowly but surely, Russia grew into an incredibly vast and powerful empire. By the mid-16th century CE, Russia was ruled by the powerful and ruthless tsar (emperor) Ivan the Terrible.[5] After Ivan the Terrible died, a very turbulent period for Russia ensued, with numerous tsars coming and going (quite often due to assassinations). Still, the great eastward expansion of Russia progressed steadily. With the rise of the Romanovs and Peter the Great, Russia's vitality grew further, epitomized

---

[5] DE MADARIAGA, Isabel. *Ivan the Terrible.* Yale University Press, 2006.

in the 1721 declaration of the Russian Empire and the coronation of Peter the Great.[6] Since Ivan the Terrible, Russian rulers referred to themselves as "tsars," meaning "emperor." Russia was *de facto* an empire for quite some time before Peter the Great, but he changed Russia for the better in numerous ways, making significant territorial expansions and fostering cultural links between Russia and Europe, hence the importance of the 1721 declaration.

The Russian Empire in the early 18th century.
By Gabagool - Own work, CC BY 3.0,
https://commons.wikimedia.org/w/index.php?curid=6617882

The Romanovs continued to rule for the next two hundred years, with powerful individuals such as Catherine the Great making important contributions.[7] However, as the 19th century rolled on, the anachronistic quality of the Russian Empire was becoming increasingly evident.

Revolutions had been shaking Europe and America for quite some time. Oliver Cromwell abolished the monarchy and had King Charles I executed in 1649, establishing a new republican system named the Commonwealth of England.[8] The American Declaration of Independence was signed in 1776, propelling the US into its incredibly successful republican era. The French had their own revolution in 1789,

---

[6] ANISIMOV, Evgeniĭ Viktorovich. *The reforms of Peter the Great: progress through coercion in Russia.* ME Sharpe, 1993.

[7] DE MADARIAGA, Isabel. *Catherine the Great.* Macmillan Education UK, 1990.

[8] England had parliamentary institutions for quite some time before Cromwell's revolution and soon experienced a restoration of monarchic sympathy.

which, together with the American Revolution, shook the whole world.[9] European monarchies were losing their foothold, and never was it so plain than in 1848. A revolutionary flame swept across Europe, only to again be extinguished, this time in part by the Russian Empire. It considered the 1848 revolutions a direct threat to its integrity and thus rushed to help its fellow monarchies in Europe.

Unfortunately for the Russian monarchy, the revolutionary sentiment—a kind of religious zeal—finally reached Russia by the middle of the 19th century. And once it reached Russia, it couldn't be eradicated. We'll now glance at the most important personalities in these early days of the revolutionary struggle in Russia.

Early Revolutionary Idealism

One of the early revolutionary attempts was linked to the so-called Decembrists, a group of mainly Russian army officers with a penchant for revolutionary thinking.[10] In the early 19th century, Emperor Alexander I ruled. Although he did start some important reforms in the Russian Empire, most of the population were still peasants dwelling in perpetual serfdom. More had to be done, and a group of broad-minded officers (or, better put, several loosely-related groups) started assembling under people such as Pavel Pestel and Nikita Muravyov.[11]

The Decembrists were inspired by the American and French Revolutions, aiming to abolish serfdom completely and perhaps also the monarchy. The Decembrists thought they had the perfect opportunity for a revolution when Emperor Alexander I died in 1825. They used the post-Alexander I confusion about who would inherit the throne to attempt a coup, which was swiftly crushed; all responsible were punished.

The Decembrists could not make a significant change for the better and may have made the monarchy even more paranoid. The Petrashevsky Circle, a circle primarily active in the 1840s that gathered intellectuals like Fyodor Dostoevsky, was closely surveilled by the

---

[9] Like Cromwell's revolution, the French Revolution was soon followed by a reinvigoration of monarchic sympathy.

[10] KIIANSKAIA, O. I. Decembrists in Russian History and Historiography: Polemical Notes. *Rossiia i sovremennyi mir*, 2017, 2: 95.

[11] O'MEARA, Patrick. *The Decembrist Pavel Pestel: Russia's First Republican*. Springer, 2016.

government. Finally, several its members were imprisoned. The Petrashevsky Circle wasn't revolutionary in the strictest sense of the word. Still, its members did read books and discuss ideas that were banned by Emperor Nicholas I.

One member of the Petrashevsky Circle, a certain Nikolay Speshnev, adopted a much more nihilistic and ruthless outlook on the revolution.[12] However, Speshnev, like Nikolay Stavrogin from Dostoevsky's *Demons*, never incited serious revolutionary action.

But a new kind of man appeared, seemingly without regard for the distinction between right and wrong, with only one goal: total abolishment of monarchy and total revolution. One such man was Sergey Nechayev (or Nechaev), the writer of the now famous *Catechism of a Revolutionary*.[13] ("Catechism" refers to Christian religious teaching, an unavoidable part of education in 19th-century Russia.) According to Sergey Nechayev, a real revolutionary must be like a religious fanatic, blindly following the "commandments" he laid out. Here's a short excerpt from his *Catechism*:

"The revolutionary is a doomed man. He has no personal interests, no business affairs, no emotions, no attachments, no property, and no name. Everything in him is wholly absorbed in the single thought and the single passion for revolution. (...) The revolutionary knows that in the very depths of his being, not only in words but also in deeds, he has broken all the bonds which tie him to the social order and the civilized world with all its laws, moralities, and customs, and with all its generally accepted conventions. He is their implacable enemy, and if he continues to live with them it is only in order to destroy them more speedily."

---

[12] TROYAN, N. The Philosophical Opinions of the Petrashevsky Circle. *Philosophy and Phenomenological Research*, 1946, 6.3: 363-380.

[13] Available at: https://theanarchistlibrary.org/library/sergey-nechayev-the-revolutionary-catechism

Sergey Nechayev.
By Unknown, but it is safe to assume he/she was dead by 1940 (i.e., 70 years ago). - http://on-island.net/History/Nechaev/SNechaev/, *Public Domain,*
https://commons.wikimedia.org/w/index.php?curid=8462592

In a way, the *Catechism of a Revolutionary* sounds more like the ramblings of a disillusioned, nihilistic youth than the writings of a serious revolutionary. Even the chief ideologue of anarchism, Mikhail Bakunin, in the end distanced himself from the obviously deranged and feverishly devoted Nechayev.[14] The life of Sergey Nechayev was turbulent, full of treachery and less-than-laudable deeds concordant with his main principle: the ends justify the means. Like many revolutionaries after him (Lenin most importantly), Nechayev was born in good conditions compared to how most other Russians lived in 1847. At the very least, his family was procured him a good basic education. Soon enough, Nechayev was a private tutor, moving to Moscow and then St. Petersburg.

It was at St. Petersburg University that Nechayev met like-minded youth. By 1868, he was deeply involved in secret plotting against the government.[15] Early in 1869, he fled abroad, possibly attempting to

---

[14] BAKUNIN, Mikhail Aleksandrovich. *God and the State*. Courier Corporation, 1970.

[15] KARAKASIS, Georgios, et al. The Catechism of Destruction: Sergei Nechaev and the spirit of Nihilism.

garner support for his cause and go under the radar of Russian authorities, who perhaps had taken note of the rowdy young revolutionary. There he met Mikhail Bakunin, who was at first amazed by Nechayev's energy and enthusiasm for the revolutionary cause. The two exchanged ideas, and Nechayev likely obtained some funds to foster the revolution back in Russia.

That same year, he returned to Russia and continued plotting against the government. His group grew bigger and bigger. Growing increasingly disillusioned about the whole project, a member named Ilya Ivanov decided to leave the group—and that's when Nechayev got an opportunity to test his ends justify the means motto. Ivanov was a threat to the revolution, and in late 1869, Nechayev's group killed Ivanov and hid his body under a thick layer of ice near Moscow. When the authorities discovered the body, the circle around Nechayev became increasingly tight. He left Russia once again and flew to Switzerland and Bakunin. During this brief period, he wrote *The Fundamentals of the Future Social System*, the system which amazed everyone for its crudeness and authoritarianism, governed by the all-mighty committee. This "future system" was ridiculed by Marx and Engels as "barracks communism." Little did everyone know that in less than fifty years, Lenin would implement the same sort of "barracks communism" foreseen by Nechayev.

Increasingly paranoid and employing his principles consistently, Nechayev became wary of Bakunin and his entourage—so much that he began gathering evidence against Bakunin to use should the need arise. This was soon discovered, and after 1870, Nechayev became increasingly isolated in the revolutionary universe. Not only Bakunin but all members of the First International distanced themselves from the feverish revolutionary. Nechayev was finally arrested in 1872 in Switzerland and extradited to Russia, where he died in prison in 1882.

While Nechayev was serving his sentence, an organization was being formed, the People's Will (or People's Freedom). Nechayev, being in prison, missed some of the most drastic actions of the People's Will.[16] Members of the People's Will, rightfully referred to as terrorists, attempted to assassinate members of the government on many

---

[16] Nicholas, I. (2014). ALEXANDER II OF RUSSIA (1818-1881). *Famous Assassinations in World History: An Encyclopedia [2 volumes]*, 12.

occasions, usually employing powerful bombs. In 1881, Alexander II was killed by Ignaci Hryniewiecki, a member of the People's Will. As Alexander II left his residence in his carriage, heading to oversee a military ceremony, Nicholas Rysakov, another young revolutionary, threw a bomb under the emperor's carriage. The emperor emerged relatively unscathed, his robust carriage withstanding the explosion.

However, as the emperor exited his carriage and tried to help those injured by the explosion, Ignaci Hryniewiecki emerged from the crowd and threw another bomb. This time, there was nothing to protect Alexander II, and the emperor soon died, his stomach and legs shattered to pieces.

Assassination of Alexander II.
https://commons.wikimedia.org/w/index.php?curid=3743278

Many other important officials were also assassinated. The radicalization sought by Nechayev was happening, but there were no concrete political achievements. For the time being, the Russian monarchy remained firmly in place. Even worse, the reform movement spurred by Alexander II, who in 1861 abolished serfdom in Russia, thus at least symbolically ending the feudal system, was essentially stopped and less reform-minded individuals replaced the office of Alexander II. Ironically, a man who abolished serfdom and planned further reforms was killed by revolutionaries who were enthusiastic, impatient, and young enough to demand instant changes. It is likely that on the day of his assassination, Alexander II would have approved Loris-Melikov's reform plan, which would have introduced a house of commons into legislative bodies. After he was assassinated, Alexander III, a much more autocratic leader, came to power.

It soon became clear that something else must be done and that assassinations wouldn't be able to dismantle the whole system. Terrorist-nihilist cells continued to plan further actions. One such cell was led by a certain Aleksandr Ulyanov.[17] Ulyanov came from a small city on the Volga River named Simbirsk, around 700 kilometers east of Moscow. He was from a well-standing family, both his mother and father being highly-educated teachers. Aleksandr excelled academically, and by 1886 (at age twenty), he had already met many students at St. Petersburg University who shared his extremist ideas.

Aleksandr and his group made some bombs and planned to assassinate Emperor Alexander III, but they were discovered by the secret police. The leaders of the plot, Aleksandr included, were hanged in 1887. The event, although seemingly insignificant at the time, extremely shook a man named Vladimir Ulyanov, who would soon become the famous Lenin. Vladimir Ulyanov was Aleksandr's younger brother, and the hanging of Aleksandr perhaps served as the final motive that made a revolutionary young boy into a professional revolutionary. But before we describe Lenin more closely, let's turn to the man he despised the most: Tsar Nicholas II Romanov.

---

[17] POMPER, Philip. *Lenin's brother: the origins of the October Revolution*. WW Norton & Company, 2010.

Chapter 2: The Last Tsar: Nicholas II

Nicholas II Romanov, born in 1868, had the ill fortune of witnessing some exceedingly turbulent times.[18] Had he ruled 100 years earlier, he would have simply been a typical Russian tsar— deeply religious, traditional, and a bit autocratic. Unfortunately, he is known as the tsar who brought Russia to its knees and couldn't do anything but watch his country fall apart.

Young Nicholas II Romanov, then tsarevich, heir to the throne (1880s).
https://commons.wikimedia.org/w/index.php?curid=16027267

---

[18] FERRO, Marc. *Nicholas II: Last of the Tsars*. Oxford University Press on Demand, 1995.

Nicholas II Romanov was profoundly influenced by his grandfather's death and the subsequent revival of authoritarianism by his father, Alexander III. (He probably witnessed the immediate aftermath of the assassination of Alexander II). Thus, in a way, the plan of the anarchists had worked: they radicalized the ruling dynasty, making life harder for everyone in Russia, which in turn precipitated a widespread revolution. The last two tsars, Alexander III and Nicholas II, lacked the reformist zeal of Alexander II and brought Russia to the brink of a civil war. Even in the 19th century, the Russian Empire was a relic of the past. Unlike European powers such as the UK, France, and Germany, the Russian economy mostly relied on rudimentary agriculture. Moreover, the power and social influence of the elites, despised by revolutionaries, was significant even after the abolition of serfdom. Until 1861, most peasants in Russia were owned by feudal landlords—members of nobility.

The emancipation reform of 1861 slightly improved this deplorable situation. However, the basic inequalities remained. The elites maintained their social status and lavish lifestyles, and peasants were obliged to take loans from the state to buy land from ex-feudal lords, which they could hardly return. Besides, the reform was slow to be implemented across the vast Russian lands, encountering numerous difficulties. The growing public frustration with Alexander II, and more generally the whole system, thus isn't surprising.

But there was quiet before the storm. Apart from witnessing the cruel death of Alexander II, Nicholas II must have had an idyllic childhood. His marriage also started rather idyllically. Nicholas II met his future wife, then Princess Alix in 1884, when he was sixteen and she only twelve.[19] The pair reunited in 1889 and finally became engaged in 1894. Sometime between these two events, Nicholas II traveled the world—from Egypt to Singapore and farther—had a dragon tattooed on his arm, and nearly died in Japan when a policeman tried to kill him with a sword.[20] As a side note, Nicholas II was deeply shaken by this event, and from then on wasn't exactly fond of Japanese people. He was, for instance, prone to dismissing their abilities due to their small build, and

---

[19] KING, Greg. *The Last Empress: The Life and Times of Alexandra Feodorovna, Tsarina of Russia*. Birch Lane Press, 1994.

[20] KOWNER, Rotem. Nicholas II and the Japanese body: Images and decision-making on the eve of the Russo-Japanese War. *The Psychohistory Review*, 1998, 26.3: 211.

these biases probably affected his decision-making during the Russo-Japanese War.

Nicholas at Nagasaki, 1891.
https://commons.wikimedia.org/w/index.php?curid=1368762

Crucially, Nicholas II wasn't acquainted with the details of leading such a large state as Russia. His father was still young, and it was expected that Nicholas II would become tsar much later.

However, Nicholas's father died in 1894, which meant that the young (twenty-six-year-old) and inexperienced Nicholas II would have to step up to the throne.[21] Things didn't start well, and each year seemed to bring something even worse. In 1896, the official coronation ceremony was held. Thousands of people flocked to Moscow to see their dear emperor and beautiful empress. Instead of a beautiful ceremony, numerous people witnessed a much worse thing: their own death. Today, the event is known as the Khodynka Tragedy.[22, 23] The tsar

---

[21] LOWE, Charles. *Alexander III of Russia*. London: W. Heinemann, 1895.

[22] Although there must have been substantial hate toward the monarchy (Nikolas II in particular), many people admired the tsar. Even more respected him for his love of tradition and quiet family life.

[23] KING, Greg; ASHTON, Janet. 'A Programme for the Reign': Press, Propaganda and Public Opinion at Russia's Last Coronation. *Electronic British Library Journal*, 2012, 1-27.

promised free food, drinks, and gifts for anyone who came to the coronation ceremony. Thousands arrived early, expecting to grab the best spots. Tight spaces, large crowds, heat, and rumors of luxurious gifts aroused the crowd so much that control wasn't possible. The result was that thousands of people were trampled to death. This was an incredibly dark omen of things to come.

Engagement photo of Nicholas II and his wife Alexandra (Princess Alix of Hesse and by Rhine, later Empress Alexandra Feodorovna).
https://commons.wikimedia.org/w/index.php?curid=5325289

It didn't help that the royal family seemed to brush aside the severity of the situation and continued with the ceremony as if nothing happened. The tsar attended the scheduled ball that night, further spurring rumors about his callousness and wickedness. The tsar was likely overwhelmed by the many ceremonies he was supposed to attend and didn't know how to respond to such an unexpected and tragic event as a deadly stampede.

The Khodynka Tragedy.
https://commons.wikimedia.org/w/index.php?curid=3739810

In the first few years of the 20th century, Russia attempted to introduce a series of agrarian reforms to ease the peasants' situation. You may recall that the abolition of serfdom granted to peasants by Emperor Alexander II didn't exactly solve all their issues. Most peasants were caught in a vicious circle of debt, forced to take loans from the state to buy their land from old feudal lords. This is why, in 1906, a series of reforms started to take place, grouped under the name of the first Prime Minister of the Russian Empire, Pyotr Stolypin.[24]

Peasants, attuned to life in a commune and facing numerous financial difficulties, were mostly collective owners of the land. For this reason, they developed a sense of togetherness and were more likely to rebel, as the Revolution of 1905 has shown. So, Stolypin wanted to encourage individual land ownership, hoping to build a solid wealthy peasant class, which would be the tsar's main stronghold in villages. Stolypin's reforms

---

[24] KOTSONIS, Yanni. The Problem of the Individual in the Stolypin Reforms. *Kritika: Explorations in Russian and Eurasian History*, 2011, 12.1: 25-52.

also made colonization, or the "Russification" of Russian Asia, much easier. In this respect, Stolypin's reforms were more successful, encouraging millions of Russians to move east.

On the international front, things were somewhat calmer. Russia kept the *status quo* with most of its former adversaries such as Turkey, Austria-Hungary, and Germany, and was on fairly good terms with France and the UK. However, by 1904, animosities with Japan reached their peak, and a war started.[25]

Japan may seem like an unlikely adversary, but in the early 20th century, Russia had a fairly aggressive eastward expansion agenda, trying to cast its influence as far as Manchuria and Korea (taking advantage of a very weak Chinese Empire), which Japan considered its areas of influence. Moreover, in 1904, the Russian fleet was dangerously close to Japan, stationed in Port Arthur in Manchuria. Japan's attack was sudden and preemptive, easily dealing a crippling hit to a major part of Russia's naval fleet.

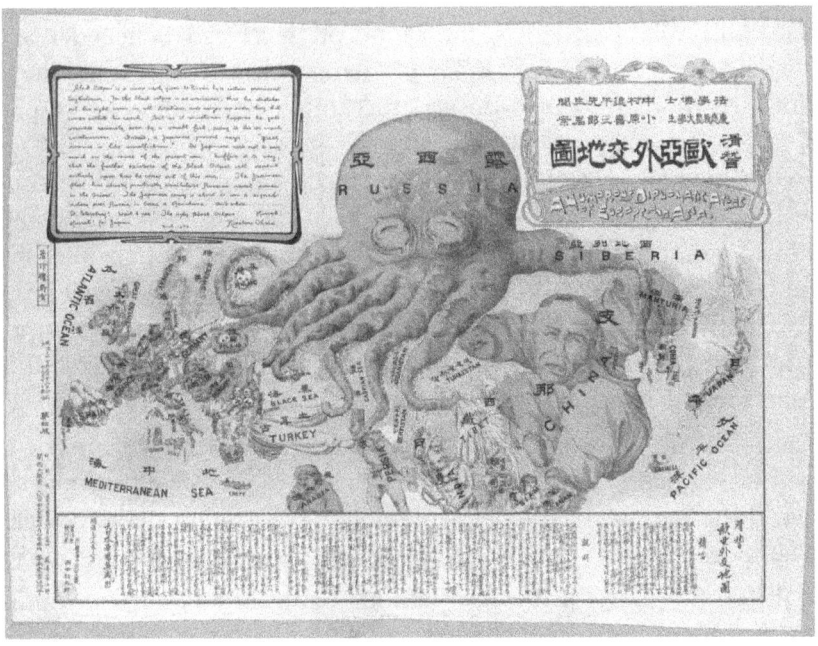

Japanese anti-Russian propaganda poster.
https://commons.wikimedia.org/w/index.php?curid=44798948

---

[25] WILSON, Sandra. *The Russo-Japanese War and Japan: Politics, Nationalism and Historical Memory.* Palgrave Macmillan UK, 1999.

Artist's depiction of the Battle of Liaoyang.
https://commons.wikimedia.org/w/index.php?curid=41019495

The Russo-Japanese War of 1904 lasted about a year and took tens of thousands of lives. Another consequence was lowered morale.[26] Back in Russia, the defeat was experienced as an embarrassment. Of course, the responsibility was ascribed to the emperor, who had believed that the war would end in Russia's favor, dangerously overestimating the readiness of Russian troops. Besides the embarrassing defeat to Japan in 1905, there was also the Bloody Sunday incident, when possibly more than 100 peaceful protestors were killed in the streets of St. Petersburg.[27] They had arrived to hand in a petition to the tsar, relating mainly to working conditions and wages. They carried religious icons and portraits of the tsar, wanting to talk directly to him about their grievances. They were welcomed with gunfire. But Nicholas II wasn't in St. Petersburg; his advisors had persuaded him not to risk facing such a large crowd with assassins lurking in the background.

From this moment, public favor decidedly shifted away from the tsar. His mistakes piled up one after another, and he was no longer the "father of the nation" or the benevolent, familial emperor. Better put, his solid support base was slowly dissipating, setting the scene for a civil war.

In 1905, the crew of the now-famous battleship *Potemkin* mutinied against its officers, an event that served as the basis for a masterpiece of

---

[26] KOWNER, Rotem (ed.). *The impact of the Russo-Japanese war.* London: Routledge, 2007.

[27] ANISIN, Alexei. The Russian Bloody Sunday Massacre of 1905: a discursive account of nonviolent transformation. *Politics, Groups, and Identities*, 2014, 2.4: 643-660.

early cinema, Eisenstein's *Battleship Potemkin*.[28] Although this mutiny was episodic and swiftly quenched by the government, it served as a sign that open conflict with authorities was possible. The failed 1905 revolution also pushed the tsarist regime into seemingly drastic reforms. Already in 1905, a draft of Russia's first constitution was made by Alexander Bulygin.[29] The tsar, who even in this decisive moment vacillated between absolutism and constitutionalism, finally accepted the October Manifesto (which included reform plans made by Bulygin). In 1906, Russia became a constitutional monarchy, with a new parliamentary body called the Duma.[30, 31] To some, it might have seemed as if the emperor's power would finally be limited by the will of the people, expressed through the Duma. But the new constitution ensured the tsar would continue having the last word. He could even dissolve the Duma whenever he saw fit. Although some of the major revolutionaries, such as Kerensky, were members of the Duma, the real revolutionary action didn't have anything to do with the tsar's parliament. What's more, hardcore revolutionaries despised the Duma as another sign of the tsar's autocracy.

---

[28] HARIHARAN, Krishnan. Eisenstein and the Potemkin Revolution. *Social Scientist*, 1979, 54-61.

[29] DULEBOHN, Jeanne Louise. *The Bulygin Duma, February-September, 1905: A Study in the History of the Russian Revolution*. University of Minnesota, 1949.

[30] MCKEAN, Robert B. The Constitutional Monarchy in Russia, 1906-17. In: *Regime and Society in Twentieth-Century Russia: Selected Papers from the Fifth World Congress of Central and East European Studies, Warsaw, 1995*. Palgrave Macmillan UK, 1999. p. 44-67.

[31] More than 100 years earlier, French King Louis XVI was in virtually the same situation. Faced with the growing dissatisfaction of almost all parts of society, he was forced to accept the formation of the National Assembly (formed a few days before the fall of Bastille on July 14, 1789) and had to accept the constitution drafted by this body. This constitution, however, kept Louis XVI as king and the most powerful man in the country. By 1792, the precarious status quo became untenable, and Louis XVI was guillotined. There are, as we can see, many parallels between the deaths of Louis XVI and Nikolai II Romanov, who was also killed soon after allowing the formation of the Duma and turning his empire into a constitutional monarchy.

Barricades in Moscow, 1905. By Unknown author,
https://commons.wikimedia.org/w/index.php?curid=24261798

Workers strike and overturn a locomotive.
https://commons.wikimedia.org/w/index.php?curid=12561948

Between the two revolutions of 1905 and 1917, a period of precarious equilibrium was made possible by slight tsarist concessions to the reformists. Strikes and protests continued but had only reached the tipping point by 1916/1917. Revolutionaries continued their almost feverish tours of vast Russia, distributing leaflets, holding secret meetings, and inciting factory workers and peasants to violently overthrow the government.

But what was happening with major professional revolutionaries, such as Lenin?

Lenin's Story

We left Lenin at the beginning of his revolutionary story: still in the shadow of his older brother, who was executed for organizing the assassination of Alexander III. Much like his older brother Aleksandr, Vladimir Ulyanov was a very good pupil.[32] The year 1887 must have been incredibly stressful for young Vladimir (seventeen at the time): he lost both his father and older brother. That year, he enrolled at Kazan University, studying law. Before long, Lenin was leading an informal group of students, organizing protests and secret meetings, and reading banned literature.

Young Lenin (around 1887).
https://commons.wikimedia.org/w/index.php?curid=49899

---

[32]HASEGAWA, Tsuyoshi. Lenin: A Biography. *Journal of Interdisciplinary History*, 2003, 33.3: 482-484.

By 1889, Lenin was a Marxist through and through. Consequently, he believed the cradle of revolution would be the proletariat—in other words, the urban working class as opposed to the peasants. In this respect, he had many opponents in Russia who believed that the impetus for social changes must come first from the peasants. At the time, they constituted an overwhelming majority of the population, as Russia was still in the initial stages of industrialization.

Lenin and fellow revolutionaries around 1897.
https://commons.wikimedia.org/w/index.php?curid=1548894

Among early Russian liberals, socialists, and anarchists, there was an archetype of the good Russian peasant. Gogol, for instance, never failed to pay his respects to the good and honorable Russian peasant, idealizing the simple life on a farm far away from the glitter of Moscow and St. Petersburg. This is nowhere more obvious than in the character Konstantin Skudronzhoglo from *Dead Souls,* a hard-working, intelligent, and honorable farm owner. Compare this representation of peaceful, honorable life on a farm to Maxim Gorky's faceless, characterless, honorless peasants who are almost always lazy, complacent, and a bit stupid. Gorky, needless to say, was deeply involved with the growing group of Marxists. Once the USSR was formed, Gorky became the most important writer in the country.

Lenin and Gorky met in 1902.[33] By that time, Lenin was already well-known in underground revolutionary movements, having been arrested and exiled by the government but never deemed a serious threat. This was an incredibly turbulent period for Lenin, who was traveling around Russia and Europe, conversing with other revolutionaries, writing articles, and distributing propaganda pieces to workers on strike. We can only imagine the feverish energy with which Lenin traveled to and from Russia, evading the Okhrana (Russian secret police) and making plans with liberals, socialists, and fellow Marxists. By 1903, a major schism appeared among Russian Marxists, who were divided between the more moderate Mensheviks (literally "those in the minority"), led by Julius Martov, and the Bolsheviks ("those in the majority"), led by Lenin. In 1912, the divorce between the Bolsheviks and Mensheviks became formal, but the two factions continued coexisting and sometimes cooperating in the joint revolutionary endeavor.[34]

The Revolution of 1905 reinvigorated Lenin and fostered his conviction that force and violence were the only way to achieve revolution. On the other hand, he wasn't convinced by the tsarist concessions or the belated formation of a constitutional monarchy and the Duma. Concessions were almost purely symbolic, with Tsar Nicholas II retaining absolute power over the Duma.

Returning to Russia, Lenin tried to incite new protests and conflicts with tsarists, to no avail. The Bolsheviks, receiving Lenin's "amen," took concrete actions, such as the 1907 Tiflis bank robbery led by none other than Joseph Stalin. But Lenin and his closest associates were soon forced to flee abroad again, fearing the Okhrana's retribution. Living a true working-class life from Switzerland, Paris, and London over to the beautiful island of Capri, Lenin had a lot of time to think about the situation. It's possible he was growing disillusioned about the whole revolutionary thing. The First World War caught him in Austro-Hungarian Poland, where Lenin reacquainted himself with Hegelianism and some classics. Moving again to the true working-class heaven of Switzerland's Zurich, Lenin could hardly believe the news of the

---

[33] YEDLIN, Tova. *Maxim Gorky: A political biography.* Greenwood Publishing Group, 1999. Available at: http://www.arvindguptatoys.com/arvindgupta/rus-gorky-biography.pdf

[34] CARR, E. H.; CARR, E. H. Bolsheviks and Mensheviks. *The Bolshevik Revolution 1917-1923: Volume One*, 1950, 26-44.

February Revolution in Russia, which prompted him to return swiftly to his motherland along with a few dozen like-minded dissidents.

This is where the "sealed train" story comes to the forefront. The German authorities recognized that Lenin and his compatriots could further destabilize Russia, their enemy, and might have helped logistically with Lenin's return to Russia. (The war was still raging, and travel to Russia from Germany or Austria-Hungary was impossible.) There were subsequently allegations that Lenin acted as a German agent with the final goal of weakening Russia and allowing Germany to take the upper hand in the war.[35] This claim came mainly from his opponents within Russia during the February Revolution. We'll never know for sure, though as soon as Lenin came to power, he made peace with the Germans (i.e., the Treaty of Brest-Litovsk signed in early 1918) in terms only acceptable to them. On the other hand, World War I was a major cause of the February Revolution, as it brought innumerable casualties, famine, disease, etc. Most of the Russian population likely wanted the war to end as soon as possible.

Having painted the landscape of pre-revolution Russia, let's take a closer look at the February Revolution.

---

[35] PHILLIPS, Steve. *Lenin and the Russian Revolution.* Heinemann, 2000. P. 27

Chapter 3: The February Revolution of 1917

On June 28, 1914, Gavrilo Princip, a young Serb from Bosnia (annexed at the time by Austria-Hungary), assassinated Franz Ferdinand, the Archduke of the Austro-Hungarian Empire and designated successor of Emperor Franz Joseph.[36] Gavrilo, a member of the Young Bosnia group (not entirely unlike the Russian anarchist groups), triggered a string of catastrophic events that caused the world to plunge into an all-out war. The catastrophe was bound to happen sooner or later. Seeing the assassination as a perfect excuse, Austria-Hungary declared war on Serbia. Virtually all European powers started mobilizing their forces soon after the assassination, and open conflicts broke out between two blocks of powers, defined well before the assassination of Franz Ferdinand in Sarajevo.

---

[36]BECHERELLI, Alberto; BIAGINI, Antenllo; MOTTA, Giovanna. Remembering Gavrilo Princip. *The First World War: Analysis and Interpretation*, 2015, 1: 17-33.

Probably the most famous depiction of the assassination of Franz Ferdinand and his wife.
https://commons.wikimedia.org/w/index.php?curid=29686990

Initially, it was believed the war would be short, but it turned out to be the biggest conflict known to mankind to that point. No country was prepared for it, and the Russian Empire was perhaps the most ill-prepared.

By 1916, the situation in Russia was abysmal, with even the most basic necessities, such as bread, becoming increasingly scarce. Strikes and protests had already become routine in Russia by 1905, and the war provided the final push that made unrest so massive that it became impossible to maintain order. What's more, those who were supposed to retain order—the army and police—were becoming increasingly disillusioned about the tsar, seeing that they might not be able to feed themselves and their families due to the government's poor decision-making.

Finally, the urban population in Russia—the proletariat working in factories—was increasing. As Russia industrialized, cities like Petrograd or

Moscow grew exponentially. For instance, in 1864, Petrograd only had around 500,000 citizens; in 1917, there were already 2,500,000 people living and working in Petrograd, most of them in newly-opened factories.[37] Although industrialization and urbanization (more specifically, the lack thereof) are often cited as one of the causes of the fall of the Russian Empire, the first steps toward industrialization were crucial in the downfall of the empire. It seems that Lenin was right in firmly believing Marx that a socialist revolution must come from the urban working class.

It is sometimes said that the February Revolution took everyone by surprise, even the professional revolutionaries. People like Lenin, absent from Russia for years, were certainly taken aback by the seemingly spontaneous February Revolution. But by 1916, just about anyone in Russia, including the government itself, knew that a violent storm was coming. Okhrana agents noticed a "state of extreme agitation of the working masses and social groups (...)."[38] The Okhrana, closely following chief agitators, socialists, anarchists, and Marxists, also noted how they helped organize protests and strikes, giving them a more concentrated and concrete political form.

One of many protests at Nevsky Prospekt in Petrograd.
https://commons.wikimedia.org/w/index.php?curid=11008740

---

[37] Britannica; Evolution of the modern city: road to revolution. Available at: https://www.britannica.com/event/July-Days

[38] MELANCON, Michael. Rethinking Russia's February Revolution: anonymous spontaneity or socialist agency?. *The Carl Beck Papers in Russian and East European Studies*, 2000, 1408: 48.; p. 6

The Okhrana also noticed a convergence between political factions, such as Bolsheviks and Narodniks, and their (and other groups') part in organizing soldiers to join riots and help form an armed uprising against the tsar.[39] The Socialist Revolutionary Party (SRP) was especially important in transferring revolutionary zeal to the army, which could always be used by the government to suffocate the unrest. Leaflets, a powerful weapon in the hands of revolutionaries, were printed on a massive scale. One such leaflet, printed and distributed by the SRP on the eve of the February Revolution, told the following story:

"You, old warriors who had begun to doubt the victory of revolution, and you, young green soldiers, haven't you felt how the whole of enormous Russia has come alert? Surely you have heard the news that is spreading."[40]

Besides Petrograd and Moscow, many other Russian cities, such as Kharkov, Saratov, Nizhny-Novgorod, Samara, and Voronezh, saw the expansion of revolutionary efforts. The most powerful impetuses came from factories. There are many memoirs of simple factory workers who participated in Bolshevik, Menshevik, and Narodnik meetings years before the February Revolution. For instance, Kapytianov tells about a 1915 Putilov factory meeting that numbered around two hundred people, where growing war-related hardships were discussed.[41] Another worker, Voronkov, remembers the formation of an informal group of like-minded socialists, anarchists, and other activists in his arsenal munition factory. This group coordinated a strike on January 9, 1916, the anniversary of the Bloody Sunday incident.

By February 14, the revolutionaries organized a massive strike, encompassing 89,000 factory workers. On this date, however, most workers simply went home. Streamlining the workers' frustration into a more violent act of rebellion was still impossible. However, on February 23, 1917 (International Women's Day), the frustration finally reached its

---

[39]Narodniks differed from Bolsheviks in their interpretation of Marx. Bolsheviks believed that the major impetus for revolution would come from the proletariat while the Narodniks focused on the *narod*—peasants—building on a tradition of glorifying peasant life. Their efforts culminated in the formation of the Socialist Revolutionary Party, perhaps the most important for the February Revolution.

[40] MELANCON, Michael. Rethinking Russia's February Revolution, p.8.

[41] Ibid., p.12

tipping point.[42] In the days leading to February 23, there were many strikes and protests, most notably textile plant workers' strikes. Finally, International Women's Day was chosen by several factories as another day of strikes, a day of great symbolic value for the whole socialist movement. Massive protests for this day might have been planned months in advance. The bread issue was a major propaganda point leading to this event. Prices had risen considerably by this time, and supply became increasingly precarious.

Thus, on February 23, 1917, tens of thousands of Petrograd factory workers and Women's Day protesters gathered in the streets, protesting the food rationing plans, demanding the end of the war and the monarchy. Women were especially vocal about the food shortage and drew more and more workers to the streets.

There was no stopping. The protests continued the next day, and likely hundreds of thousands of people roamed the streets of Petrograd. On February 25, all of Petrograd's factories were paralyzed by strikes, and the crowd on the streets grew, possibly reaching 250,000. Nicholas II urged the police to suppress the rioters with violence and gunfire, as he had done many times before. The next day, one of the regiments garrisoned in the city mutinied and clashed with the tsarist police. All the while, the tsar seemed to seriously underestimate the gravity of the situation. He frowned on increasingly desperate telegrams from Rodzianko, then Duma chairman. He wasn't even in Petrograd but in Mogilev, a city in Belarus.

By February 27, numerous regiments of the Petrograd garrison had mutinied and distributed arms among the civilian protestors, thus making the revolutionaries' complete control of Petrograd possible. The tsar couldn't even enter Petrograd by train, as rioters controlled the stations. Slowly grasping that his power had ended, Nicholas II Romanov abdicated and attempted to transfer power to his brother, Grand Duke Mikhail, on March 2. The grand duke refused, and the Romanov dynasty stepped down from the throne it had held for centuries on March 3, 1917. Nicholas II Romanov, along with his wife, four daughters, and a son, were killed in 1918 in Yekaterinburg, where they

---

[42] At the time, Russians were using the old Julian calendar, which lags thirteen days behind the newer Gregorian calendar. So, the February Revolution is more correctly the March Revolution, and the October Revolution is actually the November Revolution.

were imprisoned by the Bolsheviks.

The crowd burns symbols of the monarchy, Feb 27, 1917.
https://commons.wikimedia.org/w/index.php?curid=11008748

Protests in March, Petrograd.
https://commons.wikimedia.org/w/index.php?curid=11008738

Chapter 4: Dual Power: The Provisionals and the Petrograd Soviet

Even before the Romanovs abdicated, new institutions of power were formed: the Provisional Government, stemming from the Duma, and the Petrograd Soviet (a workers' council that also gathered soldiers who had mutinied against the tsar). [43,44] The two institutions formed *dvoyevlastiye*, literally "dual power," which signified the early rift between revolutionaries. The Provisional Government received the heritage of the Duma. It was much more moderate and often slow to act compared to the Petrograd Soviet, dominated by the Bolsheviks, which was more informal but also more extreme.

---

[43] SCHAPIRO, Leonard. The Political Thought of the First Provisional Government. In: *Revolutionary Russia*. Harvard University Press, 1968. p. 97-113.

[44] HASEGAWA, T. (1977). The Bolsheviks and the formation of the Petrograd soviet in the February Revolution. *Soviet Studies*, 29(1), 86-107.

First Provisional Government.
https://commons.wikimedia.org/w/index.php?curid=14751046

Key members of the Petrograd Soviet.
https://commons.wikimedia.org/w/index.php?curid=45602812

In an interesting twist of history, Lenin, who (contrary to Marx) believed that a revolution of the proletariat didn't need to be preceded by a bourgeois revolution, was now accusing the Provisional Government of defending bourgeois interests and advocated a complete concentration of power into the hands of the Soviet. The February Revolution was thus just a bourgeois revolution, and the proletarian revolution was still bound to happen. [45] Lenin wrote diligently and passionately against the Provisional Government. Lenin, for instance, said the following:

"The point is that Guchkov, Milyukov, Tereshchenko, and Konovalov [members of the Provisional Government] are spokesmen of the *capitalists*. And the seizure of foreign lands is necessary to the capitalists. They will receive new markets, new places to export capital to, new opportunities to arrange profitable jobs for tens of thousands of their sons, etc. The point is that at the present moment the *interests* of the Russian capitalists are identical with those of the British and French capitalists. That, and that alone, is the reason why the tsar's treaties with

---

[45] This was more likely than not another propaganda tool. Simple workers and soldiers had overthrown the tsar, but the undemocratically-elected Duma continued existing through the Provisional Government.

the British and French capitalists are precious to the Provisional Government of the Russian capitalists."[46]

Lenin's speech.
https://commons.wikimedia.org/w/index.php?curid=27944019

Thus, in Lenin's mind, the Provisionals were no different from the tsarists, who defended the same interests. As we can see, there was an ideological battle between the Provisionals and the Soviets. One of Lenin's major political points was his opposition to war since most of the Russian population wanted their country out of the war. The Provisionals, on the other hand, wanted Russia to continue waging war against Germany, and Lenin was quite adamant about their motives:

---

[46]LENIN, Vladimir. *Lenin Collected Works*, Progress Publishers, 1964, Moscow, Volume 24, pages 189-191.

"People who fan the flames of war are continuing to speak in the name of Russia. The workers and soldiers are being fed with platitudes about peace without annexations, while on the quiet a policy is being pursued which benefits only a small clique of millionaires who thrive on war."[47]

The war against Germany, in Lenin's mind, was a capitalist war, serving only the interests of the wealthy few, with poor people dying every day for these interests. This explanation, a very simple one, wasn't far from the truth and resonated with the Russian population. The reluctance of the Provisionals to stop the war was a major reason the masses were dissatisfied with the February Revolution. Lenin made sure to use this dissatisfaction to bring the Bolsheviks to the power.

Such was the revolutionary landscape of Russia in the days leading to the October Revolution. On one side was the Provisional Government led by Kerensky, perhaps from the earliest days doomed to fail due to its connection to the Duma and the tsarist regime. The Provisionals' reputation was likely stained by their previous cooperation with the regime. Now that the monarchy was fully abolished, the revolutionaries were erasing all symbols of the monarchy. Those who cooperated with the tsar (or were presented as such by Bolshevik propaganda) were the next enemy to be dealt with.

On the other side was the Soviet, much closer to factory workers, their committees, and the soldiers who had rebelled against the tsar. The Soviet, as mentioned, was largely independent of the Provisional Government (hence the term *dual power* used to describe the period between the February and October revolutions) and had much more concrete power in its hands. Soldiers and workers had ultimately brought down the tsarist regime, not the "bourgeois" members of the Provisional Government. And soon enough, they would lend their hands in bringing down the Provisionals.

---

[47] LENIN, Vladimir. *Lenin Collected Works*, Progress Publishers, 1964, Moscow, Volume 24, pages 112-114.

Chapter 5: The October Revolution of 1917

Bolshevik Rhetoric

Before we move on to describe the October Revolution and how it came about, let's focus on the ideology behind the movement, which is, simply put, Lenin's interpretation (and adjustment) of Marxism. So far, we've mentioned a few general notes on Lenin's beliefs, but now we'll deal with them in greater detail.

Lenin was a prolific writer with an immense output. Always in action, always managing, he still wrote two major books by 1909: *The Development of Capitalism in Russia* in 1899 and *Materialism and Empirio-criticism* in 1909.[48, 49] Before, after, and between writing these books, Lenin wrote countless articles for journals, opinion pieces on, say, policies of the Communist International, and even more letters (often as serious as his books and articles). You may have noticed that we emphasized the stark contrast between Lenin's lifestyle (i.e., traveling across Europe, often to luxurious destinations, and not doing any manual labor) and the lifestyle of the people whose support he mustered (blue-collar workers). It is true, however, that Lenin was a tireless worker in his own way. He considered writing his own factory and pen and

---

[48] Available at: https://www.marxists.org/archive/lenin/works/cw/pdf/lenin-cw-vol-03.pdf

[49] Available at: https://www.marxists.org/archive/lenin/works/cw/pdf/lenin-cw-vol-14.pdf

paper his hammer and sickle. He was also a great erudite, which never fails to show in his works.

In *The Development of Capitalism in Russia*, Lenin starts with a concise description of core Marxist ideas: the evolution of societies from a natural economy to a commodity and capitalist economy and the significance of the social division of labor for this evolution. For starters, a natural economy is made of homogenous societal units, where "(...) each such unit engaged in all forms of economic activity, from the acquisition of various kinds of raw material to their final preparation for consumption." [50] As the social division of labor progresses, socioeconomic units become increasingly diverse, making a firm basis for the typical capitalist economy. In this way, products become commodities and enter a complex market interplay of "use values" and "exchange values." In fact, in capitalist economies, the exchange value, expressed in money, takes priority over use values. The social division of labor necessitates the transformation of all products into exchange values because single units of society are increasingly dependent on each other for basic subsistence and growth.

The social division of labor also reduces the agricultural population and a sharp increase in the number of people working in industry. Within a natural (and to some extent, commodity) economy, it is still possible for workers to own the means of production. But as the social division of labor progresses, workers are less likely to own the means of labor. The capitalists own the means of production, while the workers have no choice but to sell their labor power.

An acidic, arrogant, and disdainful criticism of Narodniks exudes from Lenin's introduction to his first major work. Narodniks have their "romantic prejudices" (i.e., their sympathy for the peasants) and are unaccountable.[51] Any kind of communication with them is impossible, and Lenin will never cede even an inch of his theoretical territory to the Narodniks (or any other political group, for that matter). Even from the early days, it is evident just how convinced Lenin was about being one of Marx's prophets, one of those chosen to spread the wisdom of the supreme Marx to the masses.[52] Needless to say, Lenin religiously cites

---

[50] *The Development of Capitalism in Russia*, pp. 37-38.

[51] *The Development of Capitalism in Russia*, p. 42.

Marx on virtually every page of his book.

Of course, the constant mantra of Marxists, the "means of production," figures prominently in the introduction to *The Development of Capitalism in Russia*. The chief problem with capitalism is that the means of production (e.g., machines, factories, etc.) is in the hands of individual capitalist entrepreneurs who are largely to blame for the situation workers find themselves in: "And as it is a matter of the utmost indifference to the individual entrepreneur what kind of article he produces—every product yields a 'revenue.'"[53] This indifference, coupled with a focus on increasing one's own capital, leads to the basic contradiction of capitalism, according to Marx:

"Contradiction in the capitalist mode of production: the labourers as buyers of commodities are important for the market. But as sellers of their own—labour-power—capitalist society tends to keep them down to the minimum price."[54] In other words, capitalist entrepreneurs don't care about their workers or care about them only as long as they allow for the increase of capital. This basic injustice profoundly struck Lenin and fueled him with the kind of feverish energy necessary for realizing a revolution.

In *Materialism and Empirio-criticism*, written in 1908, Lenin elaborately explains the bases of the Bolshevik Party and how Bolsheviks differ from other groups, such as Mensheviks. In this book, we encounter a much angrier and more aggressive Lenin, who defends orthodox Marxist thought from the onslaught of Russian intellectuals who dared to adjust or, God forbid, criticize Marx's and Engels' thoughts. This book is interesting because it perfectly represents Lenin's way of arguing and how he put his intellectual opponents down. In the preface to the first edition of the *Materialism and Empirio-criticism*, Lenin immediately refers to Marxists who don't agree with him as "would-be Marxists" and goes on to frame their (serious) works on Marxism as "devoted mainly and almost exclusively to attacks on dialectical materialism."[55] In true Cheka and NKVD fashion, Lenin sees

---

[52] Lenin was indeed an expert on Marx, having also translated some Marx's works to Russian from the original German.

[53] Ibid. p.56.

[54] MARX, Karl, *Das Kapital*, II, 303.

[55] *Materialism and Empirio-criticism*, p. 19.

criticisms of Marx and Engels where they weren't intended and goes to serious lengths to prove that intellectuals like Aleksandr Bogdanov (initially a Bolshevik) were destroying the whole edifice of Marxism when they tried to adjust this ideology in light of new philosophical ideas, such as those of Ernst Mach.[56, 57] People like Bogdanov are "reactionary" and "revisionist" philosophers: they are trying to change something that's already perfect and truthful, and in doing so, they are undermining the revolution. The disproportion between the nature of the situation and Lenin's thinly-veiled anger is obvious and even strange, likely coming from a dark psychological place and his inability to tolerate those who didn't agree (even if only partially) with him.

If De Sade's philosophy is a "boudoir philosophy," Lenin's philosophy often looks like an "alehouse philosophy," especially when he tries to criticize others' viewpoints. For instance, Lenin accuses Ernst Mach of solipsism, even though one cannot find such assertions in any of Mach's works.[58] Lenin then proceeds to add more intellectual offenses: idealism, for instance, is used as an accusation and an insult. Those described as idealists are necessarily stupid, reactionary, revisionist, or even worse, similar to Bishop Berkeley—guilty of being an idealist believing in solipsism. Lenin criticizes solipsism as selfish, not acknowledging other people's viewpoints. Ironically, Lenin was rather solipsistic in interpreting Marxism: he was the only source of true Marxism, in his mind at least.

We believe it's important to represent at least a fraction of Lenin's works because they were so crucial for the formation of Bolshevik dogma and the way dissenting opinions were handled by the Bolsheviks. Astute observers must have been seriously worried by this, understanding that if the Bolsheviks came to power, the freedom of expression would suffer greatly. Sure enough, ten years after completing *Materialism and Empirio-criticism*, Lenin oversaw the formation of the first gulag-like camps, which hosted tens of thousands of politically-inappropriate persons.

---

[56] More on these secret police institutions later.

[57] Ernst Mach was an important Austrian physicist and philosopher of the 19thand early 20th centuries.

[58] *Materialism and Empirio-criticism*, p.42.

Now let's turn to the October Revolution, when Lenin and the Bolsheviks finally came to power and started shaping Russia according to the Marxist mold.

Fueled by the rhetoric presented above, the Petrograd Soviet was quickly radicalized into believing that the only way forward was to violently topple the Provisional Government. Truth be told, the Provisional Government, as it stemmed from the Duma, wasn't chosen democratically and, as such, was illegitimate. But before the Provisionals could organize the first elections in Russia, the Bolsheviks removed them from power. Unfortunately, the Bolsheviks didn't even dream of allowing the Russian people to choose their leaders.

The End of the Provisional Government

The Provisionals could do little to pull Russia out of the death spiral. Food uncertainty, war, and poor working conditions continued even after the February Revolution and the tsar's abdication. Strikes, protests, and even violent peasant uprisings became a part of everyday life in Russia.

Perhaps the thing that decidedly sealed the Provisionals' fate was their support for the continuation of the war. In turn, Lenin's opposition to war brought him much esteem among the growing anti-war group of Russians. The people—everyday, normal working people—are rarely pro-war, or at least cease being pro-war when the atrocious consequences of war become obvious.[59] Earlier, we saw Lenin's fiery anti-war rhetoric. We can only imagine the chaos of the post-February and pre-October Revolution days, with numerous little Lenins of the Petrograd Soviet running around Russia, denouncing the ugly capitalist war of the Provisionals. The so-called Kerensky offensive had failed, with the Central Powers managing to inflict disastrous counter-offensives, destroying the morale of the Russian troops and the whole population. By mid-July 1917, hundreds of thousands of demonstrators were gathering on the streets of Petrograd, urging the government to stop the war. At this point, the Provisional Government showed it could be as

---

[59] By the end of 1917, Russia lost millions of soldiers, their total death count rising to around 3.4 million, with up to five million more injured. Russia in 1917 had a large population (around 175 million); nevertheless, most war casualties were young men who would normally go on to work in industry or agriculture. But the effect of the war was also emotional, and people (in all of Europe, in fact) wanted senseless killing to end.

oppressive as the tsarist regime. Between July 16 and 20, possibly hundreds of demonstrators were killed, and the unrest in Petrograd was stopped, at least temporarily.[60, 61]

Violent repression of July protests.
https://commons.wikimedia.org/w/index.php?curid=2686129

The Bolsheviks were either incapable of streamlining the protests to a total revolution or (more likely, were unprepared for such a resurgence of revolutionary spirit in the capital. Lenin had made his stance on the Provisional Government clear a few months before, calling them "bourgeois" and "capitalists." Because of their reluctance during the tumultuous July days, the Bolsheviks reached one of their lowest points. The Provisionals finally cracked down on the Bolsheviks, who became an illegal, underground party. Lenin was forced to flee to Finland, and Trotsky was arrested. Even more importantly, Bolshevik propaganda tools—their printing presses—were destroyed, and their *Pravda* (Justice) newspaper was made illegal.

This only slowed down the work of Bolsheviks, who were well-versed in underground actions, having worked for years under the tsarist

---

[60] The demonstrators themselves were violent, having inflicted significant damage on the government forces.

[61] RABINOWITCH, Alexander. *Prelude to revolution: The Petrograd Bolsheviks and the July 1917 uprising.* Indiana University Press, 1991.

regime. The final push for the October Revolution came from the Kornilov coup. This coup was probably an expression of the anger and frustration felt by everyone in the Russian army, at its peak after the shameful end of Kerensky's July offensive.[62]

The news of General Lavr Kornilov's army nearing Petrograd brought fear to the capital, especially to the Petrograd Soviet, against whom Kornilov's frustration was aimed.[63] The Bolsheviks had connections everywhere and slowed the advance of Kornilov by sabotaging his telegraph communication and railroad transport. The Bolsheviks (and other parties of the Soviet) also had connections among Kornilov's army and swayed many soldiers to abandon the march toward Petrograd. The Provisionals were, in fact, so frightened by the advance of Kornilov that they reversed their recent ban on Bolsheviks and—even more important—supported the far-left parties, hoping to obtain their support.

By September 13, it became evident that Kornilov couldn't overthrow the government, and the affair reached its end. If Lenin hadn't felt the time was ripe for a violent, armed rebellion against the government in July, now he was feeling more confident. A plan was being made on how the Provisionals would soon be overthrown. Everyone in Petrograd knew that something big was being prepared. The Provisionals, weak from the outset and almost completely incapable of concrete action, could only watch as the Bolsheviks planned their final attack.

On October 24 (November 6, Gregorian calendar), they tried to inflict a crippling blow to the Bolsheviks by raiding the headquarters of *Worker's Path* newspaper. However, they only succeeded in pushing the Bolsheviks to start their armed uprising. The Bolsheviks quickly retook the *Worker's Path* building, and on October 25, Central Telegraph came under the control of the Bolsheviks. It's rather symbolic that the seizing of power started by gaining full control of communications within the city. The Bolsheviks were always masters of propaganda, and even though their armed forces finally outnumbered the Provisionals' forces,

---

[62] It's possible, however, that at some point, Kerensky thought it necessary to further strengthen the Provisional Government with army support and invited Kornilov to bring an army to Petrograd. The general feeling, however, was that an enemy army was marching toward Petrograd, attempting to take power by force.

[63] ASCHER, Abraham. The Kornilov Affair. *Russian Review*, 1953, 12.4: 235-252.

the Bolsheviks knew it was still imperative to first gain control of communications and then continue with the rest.

Red Guards, workers of Vulkan factory (October 2017).
https://commons.wikimedia.org/w/index.php?curid=4283360

The Bolsheviks took strategic locations easily. The Winter Palace, although defended by a handful of soldiers loyal to the government, was ultimately taken by the Bolsheviks on October 26.[64] Soon, the Bolsheviks had taken the most important locations in Moscow and other major cities in Russia. The Provisionals were all imprisoned apart from Kerensky, who managed to flee, attempting to gather forces and attack the Bolsheviks.

At this time, there was a curious attempt to conduct the first democratic elections in Russia. At best, these must have been partial elections due to the challenges of organizing in the middle of a war with a population of over one hundred million. The dual power continued to exist for a short while even after the fall of the Provisionals. The Soviets continued to amass power, and the Bolsheviks dissolved the Constituent Assembly after operating only for a few days, on January 19. Unsurprisingly, the Constituent Assembly was dissolved, as the Bolsheviks only won around 23.3 percent of the votes, behind the Social Revolutionaries (around 37.6 percent). The elections painted a much

---

[64] CARR, Edward Hallett. *The Bolshevik Revolution, 1917-1923.* WW Norton & Company, 1985.

more heterogeneous picture than the one the Bolsheviks were ready to accept.

The abolishment of the first real Russian democratic institution was a powerful omen of things to come, an omen of the dictatorship of the proletariat. Marxists believe that, for the Communist utopia to be materialized, first there has to be a period of dictatorship of the proletariat. Namely, an authoritarian proletariat party has to take hold of all power and slowly lead the state toward Communist ideals, such as the abolishment of private property, common ownership of means of production, a classless system, etc. The ultimate irony is that in most places where Marxism-Leninism was applied, the dictatorship of the proletariat tended to *increase* as time passed.

Decades after the revolutions ended, countries like the USSR, the People's Republic of China, and many others were still led by an omnipotent party of influential Communists, with diminishing personal (and social) freedoms. Moreover, the dictatorship of the proletariat led to the formation of the new ruling class, the red bourgeoisie. The term *red bourgeoisie* comes from the 1968 protests of Belgrade students, who were especially vocal about the formation of the new Communist elite—in their view, contrary to real Communism. Milovan Djilas, a Yugoslav Communist once close to Tito, wrote an important book on this topic called *The New Class: An Analysis of the Communist System* (1957). Djilas correctly understood the repercussions of having a Communist elite, establishing a timeline according to which most Communist countries first go through an authoritarian period. This is followed by gradual loosening of the party's terror and establishment of a well-delineated ruling class governed primarily by self-interest and establishing dominance over other classes. This inevitably leads to stagnation as the ruling class grows more and more self-indulgent. This is exactly what happened in Djilas' native Yugoslavia and the USSR.

Dissolution of the Constitutional Assembly.
https://commons.wikimedia.org/w/index.php?curid=23515969

The Social Revolutionaries, the Narodniks, fared much better with the peasant population of Russia, still an overwhelming majority compared to the growing working-class urban population, which usually supported the Bolsheviks. While the Bolsheviks never had an overly positive attitude toward the peasants, the first elections must have sealed the peasants' fate and their status of perpetual subordination to the urban working-class proletariat. But if the Bolsheviks had reason to suspect the intentions of the peasants, their paranoia and aggression were most certainly disproportionate. Knowing how hard they worked to come to power and aware that someone else could employ their methods to do the same, the Bolsheviks knew they had to be even more ruthless than the most ruthless jailer of the tsarist regime. The Red Terror spared no one, as we'll soon see.

Chapter 6: The Red Terror

New Policies
Land Reform

With the hubbub of the October Revolution still lingering, Lenin drafted his Decree on Land, which oversaw the complete abolishment of private land ownership.[65] The Decree was a bold move, an attempt to solve an issue that plagued the tsarist and the Provisional regime: neither could solve the land question. It's safe to say that the Bolsheviks (initially supported by a significant number of Social Revolutionaries) initially focused on redistributing the land hitherto owned by the Church and the nobility. The hard question of how peasants would make peace with the fact that they didn't own the land (and, according to the Decree on Land, could not buy or sell it), was put aside. The same was true for the even more unpleasant question of how peasants would compensate the state for allowing them to live on and cultivate the land redistributed to them.

From the outset, the Bolsheviks considered the Decree on Land temporary. Lenin believed that the state of the Russian peasantry was such that it hadn't yet entered its capitalist phase, with the ultimate goal of transcending capitalism and achieving collectivism. In other words, the Bolsheviks predicted that their reform would lead to the establishment of capitalism in the countryside, with the corresponding rise of the

---

[65] CHANNON, John. The Bolsheviks and the peasantry: The land question during the first eight months of Soviet rule. *The Slavonic and East European Review*, 1988, 66.4: 593-624.

middle (self-subsisting) and wealthy peasant class, the kulaks. The inherent problems of capitalism would then force the peasants to push for their own proletarian revolution. The Decree on Land was thus a compromise between the Bolsheviks and peasants but by no means the last move of the central government.

The situation was as follows. In the revolutionary years, those in the countryside distanced themselves from the chaos of the urban centers. For instance, the peasants could hardly rely on factories for a steady supply of agricultural tools. In tumultuous times, self-preservation overpowers collective thinking, and Russian peasants had further reasons for skepticism as the land reform was referred to as temporary.[66]

Then there was the alcohol problem. Namely, the tsarist regime had banned alcohol production in 1914, attempting to curb this habit, which threatened to undermine soldiers' battle readiness (among other things).[67] Illegal alcohol production skyrocketed, a significant proportion of which came from agricultural products that should have been used for food. And finally, there was the food supply problem in 1918, coupled with the civil war and revolts sparking across the country.

All this added up to the almost impossible task of bringing grain from the periphery to the industrial centers of Russia. The government also had to coax peasants into handing over grain. For instance, they tried to establish an exchange of products: industrial centers sent over tools, and peasants sent grain. This may have been a good idea, but in the end, the centers didn't receive enough grain, and the Bolsheviks had to resort to the forced requisition of grain. This, in turn, sparked revolts all over the country. Anyone who didn't want to hand over the amount of grain the Bolsheviks (who from mid-1918 named themselves "Communists") demanded was a potential traitor and a target for the Red Terror and its Nazgûl division, the Cheka. These were all major reasons behind the Red Terror in the countryside.[68]

---

[66] Ibid.

[67] HERLIHY, Patricia. The Russian Vodka Prohibition of 1914 and Its Consequences. *Dual Markets: Comparative Approaches to Regulation*, 2017, 193-206.

[68] MELGUNOFF, Sergei. The Record of the Red Terror. *Current History (1916-1940)*, 1927, 27.2: 198-205.

Crucial members of the early Cheka: from left to right, Peters, Unszlicht, Belenky, Dzerzhinsky, Menzhinsky.
https://commons.wikimedia.org/w/index.php?curid=3200226

War Communism

This approach was increasingly used from mid-1918 when impending economic difficulties could no longer be ignored or downplayed. War Communism was an authoritarian attempt to control the economy during the tumultuous Russian Civil War period.[69] The most important aspects of War Communism were the nationalization of industry, a ban on strikes, obligatory work when necessary (i.e., the inauguration of the Gulag system), grain requisition, food rationing, and a ban on private enterprises.

The previously-presented land reform and the requisition of grain produced a vicious cycle. Peasants were discouraged from producing surplus grain, knowing the state would take it anyway. But grain had to be requisitioned, and it didn't matter if the peasants didn't have enough to eat.[70] The most severe consequence of War Communism is certainly

---

[69] MALLE, Silvana. *The economic organization of War Communism 1918-1921*. Cambridge University Press, 2002.

[70] The Bolsheviks, of course, were faced with a war on two fronts. Either they would requisition grain from the peasants and face peasant unrest or they would leave cities without bread and risk

the Russian famine of 1921-1922, when millions (probably around five million) died.[71] This famine resulted from numerous factors, with drought and bad harvests complementing the catastrophic Communist policies. The chaos of the civil war, burning and looting, and reprisals from the Reds and Whites sealed the fate of millions of Russians, who were doomed to starve. The situation was so bad that people resorted to cannibalism, and not in isolated cases. In their attempt to bring a new form of society to the Russian people, the Bolsheviks degraded them to a state where only inhumanity guaranteed survival. Moreover, they only allowed foreign aid once the famine progressed so much that it threatened the country's stability.

Red Terror

It's safe to say that the full-blown Red Terror started with the formation of the Cheka (*Vserossiyskaya chrezvychaynaya komissiya*, abbreviated VChK, which then became "Cheka").[72] The tsarist Okhrana was notorious for its methods and terror sown across Russia, and the Cheka would take this notoriety to another level. Numerous revolutionaries noted the incapacity of the Okhrana. Lenin, Stalin, and their numerous associates were arrested multiple times and exiled. Still, their penitentiary sojourns seemed like nice vacations compared to how the Cheka and later NKVD treated its prisoners/victims.[73] The revolutionaries likely believed that what Russia needed wasn't *more freedom* but even less freedom. Fueled by counterrevolutionary paranoia and terrorized by ubiquitous reactionary forces, the Bolsheviks consciously adopted the example of the Jacobin Terror from the French Revolution, eliminating anyone who dared speak against them.[74]

---

a reinvigoration of protests and strikes and the loss of their most solid support base: the urban working class.

[71] WILLIAMS, Christopher. The 1921 Russian famine: Centre and periphery responses. *Revolutionary Russia*, 1993, 6.2: 277-314.

[72] LAUCHLAN, Iain. Guardians of the People's Total Happiness: The Origins and Impact of the Cult of the Cheka. *Politics, Religion & Ideology*, 2013, 14.4: 522-540.

[73] NKVD comes from *Narodný komissariat vnutrennih del,* which can be translated as People's Commissariat for Internal Affairs.

[74] Trotsky is said to have compared Lenin with Robespierre.

In the basements of the Cheka.
https://commons.wikimedia.org/w/index.php?curid=65236538

Escort of prisoners.
https://commons.wikimedia.org/w/index.php?curid=65236526

According to Martin Latsis, who was at the top of the Ukrainian branch of the Cheka, the essence of the Red Terror consisted of the following:

"We are not waging war against individual persons. We are exterminating the bourgeoisie as a class. During the investigation, do not look for evidence that the accused acted in deed or word against Soviet power. The first questions that you ought to put are: To what class does he belong? What is his origin? What is his education or profession? And it is these questions that ought to determine the fate of the accused. In this lies the significance and essence of the Red Terror."[75]

Even before the Russian Civil War gained momentum, the *modus operandi* of the Cheka was clear: total annihilation of anything that even smelled of counterrevolution. Dressed in their long leather overcoats, Chekists would soon become grim reaper figures. They had eyes and ears everywhere, and anyone could be suspected of counterrevolution, anti-Communist reaction, bourgeois interests, or being a kulak.[76]

The Red Terror may have been chaotic, haphazard, and even random, but there were clear orders from the top urging the terror to begin. For instance, on November 9, 1918, when the Cheka had already been operating for some time, Lenin said the following at a rally:

"The important thing for us is that Cheka is directly exercising the dictatorship of the proletariat, and in that respect its services are invaluable. There is no way of emancipating the people except by forcibly suppressing the exploiters. That is what Cheka is doing, and therein lies its service to the proletariat."[77]

By allowing the Cheka to wreak havoc across Russia, Lenin opened the path to the proliferation of the criminal Communist class, sadists, Machiavellians, and, to be completely straightforward, psychopaths who wouldn't let such petty things as basic humanity get in the way of their Bolshevik career. Hearing Lenin talk about Martin Latsis, whose impeccable logic regarding the *modus operandi* of the Cheka was quoted

---

[75] LATSIS, Martin, *Red Terror*, no 1, Kazan, 1 November 1918, p. 2.

[76] "Kulak" simply means a "well-standing peasant," someone with a significant amount of land who hires people to work on his land. Kulaks were opposed to many Bolsheviks reforms. They were clamped down on by the Communist government as one of the classes whose sole existence went against the revolution in the opinion of the Communist propagandists.

[77] LENIN, V. I. Collected Works. SPEECH AT A RALLY AND CONCERT FOR THE ALL-RUSSIA EXTRAORDINARY COMMISSION STAFF NOVEMBER 7, 1918, available at: https://www.marxists.org/archive/lenin/works/cw/pdf/lenin-cw-vol-28.pdf, p.170.

above, is enough to understand this class of criminal communists: "(...) One need not go to the same absurd lengths as Comrade Latsis, one of our finest, tried and tested Communists."[78] In other words, Comrade Latsis was one of the best imaginable Communists despite (or, should we say, exactly *due to*) his ruthlessness.

A slogan from the times of Red Terror, loosely translated as: "Long live Red Terror" (bottom) and "Death to the bourgeoisie."
https://commons.wikimedia.org/w/index.php?curid=28252839

It is sometimes said that the Red Terror began after a series of assassination attempts. However, it's closer to the truth that assassinations resulted from the growing Bolshevik terror. For instance, on August 11, Lenin issued the now-infamous "Hanging Order," which urged the heads of the Penza Governorate to terrorize the population of their regions to ensure the requisitioning of grain.[79] Lenin further specified that at least 100 persons must be hanged due to unrest in the Penza and the unwillingness of the population to allow their grain to be requisitioned by the Communists.

Whatever the causal chain behind the Red Terror, there were numerous attempts on Lenin's life, roughly from early 1918 onward. The first major (successful) assassination was that of Moisei Uritsky,

---

[78] Ibid. p. 389.

[79] The requisitioning was often enforced through harsh measures. As the flames of the civil war were reaching their peak, the Communist reacquisition of grain grew ever more violent. However, the Communists were not the only ones to resort to such actions.

chief of the Cheka, when he was killed by Leonid Kannegisser on August 17, 1918.[80] This was a clear message to the Bolsheviks that the dictatorship of the proletariat was becoming too much. Lenin was almost killed on August 30, 1918, by an old revolutionary, Fanny Kaplan (who battled previously against the tsarist regime).[81] As a sixteen-year-old girl, in 1906, she was involved in manufacturing a makeshift bomb to be used against tsarist officials; she was arrested and spent the next nine years in the tsarist penal systems in Siberia.

Fanny Kaplan was released after the February Revolution but quickly understood that Lenin was making an equally authoritarian system. One of the decisive events in this respect was Lenin's abolishment of the first Constituent Assembly, which Fanny stated as her main reason for attempted assassination when she was captured by the Cheka.

Fanny shot several rounds at Lenin as he stepped out of a Moscow factory, heading toward his car. Lenin was badly wounded but survived, while Fanny was swiftly executed.

This event marked the official start of the Red Terror. Perhaps initially the Bolsheviks (and, more specifically, their Cheka agents) had at least a dose of reluctance when it came to suppressing dissenting opinions. After Fanny Kaplan attempted to kill Lenin, the Chekists' violence received an official pardon, justification, and motive, bringing Russians into a new reign of terror that would only end three decades later with the death of Stalin

Another important assassination was that of German Ambassador Wilhelm Mirbach, organized and executed by the Left Socialist-Revolutionaries on July 7, 1918.[82] Maria Spiridonova, one of the top people in the Left SR, took responsibility and was soon prosecuted by the Cheka for her open opposition to the Bolshevik (Communist) regime, along with numerous other politically inconvenient individuals.[83]

---

[80] SCHNEER, Jonathan. *The Lockhart Plot: Love, Betrayal, Assassination and Counter-Revolution in Lenin's Russia*. Oxford University Press, USA, 2020.

[81] SMITH, Scott B. Who Shot Lenin? Fania Kaplan, the SR Underground, and the August 1918 Assassination Attempt on Lenin. *Jahrbücher für Geschichte Osteuropas*, 1998, H. 1: 100-119.

[82] ERICH SENN, Alfred; GOLDBERG, Harold J. The Assassination of Count Mirbach. *Canadian Slavonic Papers*, 1979, 21.4: 438-445.

[83] Maria Spiridonova was arrested and released numerous times by the Communists and was ultimately executed in 1941 at Stalin's orders, along with other political prisoners. One of those

Spiridonova and her compatriots believed that the Bolsheviks (with whom they closely collaborated until this point) had gone astray and were leading the country into chaos. She was also well-informed about the worsening situation in Russian villages and knew that violent reacquisitions took place. There were numerous uprisings against the Bolsheviks all around Russia. Even in Petrograd, the Left SR started a serious revolt (shortly after the assassination of Wilhelm Mirbach) that was, unfortunately for them, too disorganized and aimless to topple the Bolsheviks.[84] This unsuccessful revolt of the Left SR finalized the elimination of all non-Bolshevik political parties.

Melgunov's Account of the Red Terror

Sergei Melgunov was a politician allied with the Popular Socialist Party, one of the parties that entered the newly-formed Duma and later the Provisional Government. The Popular Socialist Party was influenced heavily by the Narodnik movement; it was largely free from the Marxist ideology that took over most other revolutionary parties. Popular Socialists were also somewhat milder than the Bolsheviks or the Left SRs, as they didn't condone acts of violence such as assassinations.

The Popular Socialists lost their ground after the October Revolution. Melgunov was arrested in 1919 and forced to flee Russia in 1922. While in exile, Melgunov wrote one of the most important books on the Red Terror (eponymously titled), published in 1924.[85] Melgunov's work is similar to *The Gulag Archipelago* in that it's a mixture of personal experiences, archive documents, and other people's experiences with the Red Terror. We might even say that Melgunov survived the Red Terror's first edition while Solzhenitsyn went through the second, arguably even more senseless and violent, edition. Melgunov describes it here:

"Red terror held a sword of Damocles above thousands of people. There were cases when the prisoners refused to leave their cell when

---

people was Fritz Noether, a German-Jewish mathematician who emigrated to the USSR to flee the Nazis. Einstein pleaded for the release of Noether, to no avail. In the end, Noether was killed by people like those he had run away from.

[84] HAFNER, Lutz. The Assassination of Count Mirbach and the "July Uprising" of the Left Socialist Revolutionaries in Moscow, 1918. *The Russian Review*, 1991, 50.3: 324-344.

[85] Available for free at https://ia804502.us.archive.org/28/items/RedTerrorInRussia1918-1923/S.P.Melgunov_Red_Terror_In_Russia_1918-1923_En.pdf

they were released, fearing that a summon for release was a ruse to coax them out of prison for an execution. There were other cases where people left the cell convinced that they were being released and the other prisoners hailed them with usual cheers. But a few days later the last names of the falsely released appeared in the list of the executed by firing squad. And there were many more whose names were never published."[86]

The Bolsheviks, faced with the terror and revolutionary methods they had employed just a few months earlier, vowed to retaliate even more violently. This kind of Old Testament, eye-for-eye thinking is evident in the official newsletter of the Cheka, supplied by Melgunov: "Comrades! They slap one [of] our cheek[s], and we reciprocate that threefold by slugging the whole face. A vaccination was performed, i.e., red terror ... That vaccination was performed everywhere in Russia, particularly in Morshansk, where we responded to the assassination of comrade Uritski and wounding of comrade Lenin."[87]

Something must be done, and in typical Bolshevik fashion, almost any action was better than non-action, even if that meant killing innocent people. A list of accomplished executions was at least something; it was a product of a meat-grinding machine called Cheka, a slap on the cheek of the imaginary bourgeoisie counterrevolution. It was a grim omen of the days of Stalin's purges, where execution plans were followed with *quotas*, as one would make for grain production.

In his book, Melgunov denounces the Bolshevik use of hostages, people from all walks of life. Some were connected to the old Russian nobility, others were suspected of bourgeois tendencies, and yet others were simply unfortunate enough to find themselves suspected by the Cheka. These people were held in deplorable conditions in captivity and executed when the Party needed to avenge a fallen comrade or simply provide a spectacle of power. There was an even more pernicious institution of hostage-taking: in 1918, the Cheka was already transferring guilt from "guilty" individuals to their families so that the wives, husbands, children, or parents of those initially arrested were also arrested.[88]

---

[86] Ibid. p. 24.

[87] Ibid. p. 25.

[88] Another parallel with the later terror instigated by Stalin, when it was common for whole

The Bolsheviks were particularly cruel toward peasants. Peasants were intrinsically "reactionary," and their existence (along with their lifestyle) as a class was an inconvenience, a "necessary evil" yet contradictory to the real Bolshevik way of life. Melgunov gives us an example in the Tambov Rebellion of 1920.[89] The Cheka had given clear orders to its operatives: arrest everyone older than eighteen and execute everyone if riots continued. Introduce severe taxes, and when peasants fail to pay, confiscate their lands and property. The Tambov reprisals were brutal: five villages were burnt to the ground, and 250 peasants were executed.

Melgunov also accompanies his text with images testifying of the extremely sadistic, inhumane treatment of prisoners by the Bolsheviks. Some of these images depict the corpses of tortured individuals with mutilated genitals. For these most gruesome tasks, the Cheka had to rely on some of the worst imaginable people. While the Bolsheviks would say this was only a transitory necessity (and perhaps even briefly believed this), the rise of the class of torturers, rapists, criminals, sadists, and psychopaths employed by the government continued, reaching unimaginable heights during the reign of Stalin.

Anti-religious Crimes

The Bolsheviks were aggressively anti-religious. From the October Revolution onward, religious people, communities, and institutions were systematically targeted—especially Orthodox Christians, since they were the most numerous in USSR. Thousands of priests were arrested and executed, including those in the most notable religious positions, such as bishops and archbishops. Church valuables were requisitioned by force, thousands of churches were demolished or repurposed, and religious civilians were prosecuted.

Antireligious policies intensified with the rise of Stalinism from 1928 onward. In 1931, the Cathedral of Christ the Saviour in Moscow, one of the largest Orthodox Christian buildings at the time, was demolished to make space for the Palace of the Soviets, which was never built.[90] Tens of thousands of priests were again sent to Gulags as Stalinist paranoia

---

families to be sent to Gulags after the initial arrest of one family member.

[89] SINGLETON, Seth. The Tambov Revolt (1920-1921). *Slavic Review*, 1966, 25.3: 497-512.

[90] The Cathedral of Christ the Saviour in Moscow was finally rebuilt in 2000.

reached its peak. With the start of World War II, aggressive anti-religious policies went out of focus. Today, we know that even Stalin himself, who once studied to become a priest, turned to religion to find consolation during the darkest days of the 1941 German offensive in the USSR.

Chapter 7: Civil War and the Struggle for Control

So far, we have barely mentioned organized armed resistance groups that tried to counter the progress of the Bolsheviks. The Russian Empire didn't simply become Communist overnight: The October Revolution plunged Russia into a brutal civil war that lasted for several years. The Communists were only able to take over the lands of the Russian Empire after years of fierce fighting, with millions of people finding their death on the battlefields of the Russian Civil War. Many different military groups were involved in this conflict, each with its own interests and aims.[91] Roughly speaking, we can divide them into four categories: Reds who supported the Bolshevik government, Whites mainly consisting of ex-Imperial soldiers and officers, separatists (e.g., Polish, Ukrainian, and Baltic separatists), and Anti-Bolshevik leftists (e.g., the Green Army and Makhno's army).

Red Army

The Communist-led Red Army was by far the strongest belligerent of the Russian Civil War. It was led by Leon Trotsky, one of Lenin's closest associates. Trotsky was also instrumental in the formation of the

---

[91] The landscape was similar to that of China in its concurrent Warlord Era. Namely, after the dissolution of a great empire (i.e., Russian or Chinese), a period of chaos and fragmentation ensued, with numerous small warlords taking bits and pieces of territory and posing as the chief authorities in their regions.

Red Army. Initially, the Bolsheviks relied on Red Guards, units formed on a voluntary basis consisting largely of ex-imperial soldiers and urban workers.

Immediately after the October Revolution, it became clear to Trotsky that a much larger force must be built if the Bolsheviks wanted to take over Russia entirely. Thus, peasants were conscripted into what became the Red Army.[92] Trotsky was known for his energetic, authoritative, and pragmatic style of leadership. For instance, Trotsky brought in numerous military experts, ex-tsarists, to help the formation and operation of the Red Army.

Trotsky oversaw the institution of political commissars, largely non-military personnel attached to military units who ensured that no one strayed from the communist path and supervised the work of ex-tsarist officers and experts. Rushing across Russia in his armored train, Trotsky maintained morale among the troops, delivering fiery speeches and diligently disseminating communist ideas. The man himself emphasized the importance of this train: "During the most strenuous years of the revolution, my own personal life was bound up inseparably with the life of that train. The train, on the other hand, was inseparably bound up with the life of the Red Army. The train linked the front with the base, solved urgent problems on the spot, educated, appealed, supplied, rewarded, and punished."[93]

---

[92] ERICKSON, John. The Origins of the Red Army. In: *Revolutionary Russia*. Harvard University Press, 1968. p. 224-258.

[93] TROTSKY, Leon. My life; Available at:
https://www.marxists.org/archive/trotsky/1930/mylife/ch34.htm

Leon Trotsky delivering a speech from his armored train.
https://commons.wikimedia.org/w/index.php?curid=68904732

The nascent Red Army constantly needed political reassurance and guidance, and it received a leader perfectly equipped for the job. The sullen Stalin, for instance, would never have been able to do the job Trotsky managed to do. The latter steamed through Russia, covering more than 100,000 kilometers in a few short years, motivating soldiers from the roof of his armored train and bringing deserting regiments back to the Bolshevik faith.

After the introduction of mandatory conscription, the Red Army's ranks rose to around one million by the end of 1918, its numbers steadily increasing from then on. Perhaps it wasn't the most well-equipped army of the period, but its numbers and, most importantly, revolutionary zeal were what brought it victory in the Russian Civil War. The White Armies, on the other hand, lacked a unifying ideal and were primarily bonded by a mutual animosity toward the Bolsheviks.

Cockade (depicting a hammer and plough) initially used by the Red Army, later replaced by the famous hammer and sickle cockade.
By Dmitry Baranovskiy – https://thenounproject.com/DmitryBaranovskiy/collection/hammer-sickle/, CC BY 3.0, https://commons.wikimedia.org/w/index.php?curid=78246993

The White Movement

The White Armies (Whites) weren't a coherent, well-organized group, not even by a longshot. They consisted mainly of ex-tsarist armies, led by tsarist generals, who were unified in their mutual hatred for the Bolsheviks. The most important leaders of the White movement were Lavr Kornilov (whom you may remember from the earlier mentions of the Kornilov affair/attempted coup), Anton Denikin, Pyotr Wrangel, Alexander Kolchak, and Nicholas Yudenich.[94]

Although lacking a unifying ideology and scattered across vast Russian lands, the Whites were a considerable force, at one point consisting of more than three million soldiers. Allied forces supported the Whites, as the latter opposed the Brest-Litovsk peace and would have likely restarted the war against Germany if they had had the opportunity to do so.[95] However, while the Whites didn't have a unified ideology, they did

---

[94] BORTNEVSKI, Viktor G. White Administration and White Terror (the Denikin Period). *The Russian Review*, 1993, 52.3: 354-366.

[95] HUGHES, Matthew, et al. Allied Intervention in the Russian Civil War. *The Palgrave Concise Historical Atlas of the First World War*, 2005, 98-99.

tend to believe in all sorts of conspiracies: a rumor ran through the ranks of the Whites that Jews were to blame for all the mess in Russia: namely, numerous Bolsheviks were Jews and had all sorts of satanic goals. Needless to say, this further fueled centuries-old anti-Semitism in Russia.[96] There were also talks of freemasons and how they were connected to the Jews. It is likely these rumors spread like wildfire for several reasons: historical animosity toward the Jews in Russia, the sheer uncertainty and inexplicability of the situation, and close contact between people enlisted in the army.[97] The rumors were also incited by White Army propaganda, which sought to discredit the Bolsheviks and denounce them as foreign spies.

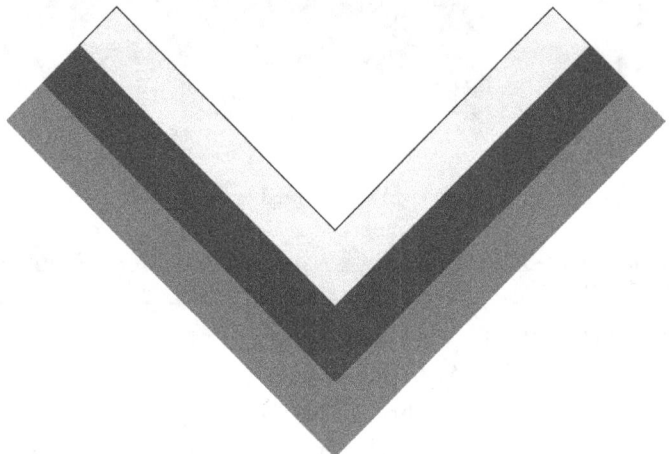

Insignia of White (Volunteer) Army.
By Thespoondragon – Own work. File:Bronepoezd ed ros.jpg, File:Бронепоезд На Москву-2.png, File:Volunteer Army infantry company.jpg, File:Denikin_poster.jpg [1], CC0, https://commons.wikimedia.org/w/index.php?curid=79507613

---

[96] BUDNITSKII, Oleg. Jews, pogroms, and the White movement: a historiographical critique. *Kritika: Explorations in Russian and Eurasian History*, 2001, 2.4: 1-23.

[97] Pogroms aimed at Jews happened quite regularly in the Russian Empire (and in other countries). It is estimated that anti-Jewish pogroms during the Russian Civil War took at least 50,000 and up to 250,000 lives. These crimes were mostly committed in Ukraine, which had a large Jewish population. The Ukrainian nationalists killed the most Jews, as the latter would be an economically powerful and numerous minority group in the future independent Ukraine. But other factions—Whites, Greens, Reds—all committed atrocities against Jews. This must be understood in the context of the Russian Civil War, which was extremely atrocious for civilians. Up to ten million (perhaps even more) civilians of all nationalities, ethnicities, and races were killed during the war.

There were voices in the White movement calling for the reinstitution of the monarchy. While this may have appealed to some Russians, it was a very bad move from the White propaganda department (not that there was one single, supreme center of White propaganda). [98] Their association to the failed regime of Provisionals served to produce a similar effect. The Whites owe their military successes and popularity primarily to the brutality of the Bolsheviks and the consequences of Brest-Litovsk. Their political choices only served to discredit their military achievements.

The Whites had significant forces in the west and south of European Russia in the regions of modern-day Ukraine, Belarus, Georgia, Azerbaijan, and Armenia, led by Denikin and Yudenich. Whites were also dispersed across Russia's far east, where some units held ground well after the civil war ended.

Anton Denikin is perhaps the most important White general. He led the ill-fated White offensive on Moscow in the summer of 1919. [99] Denikin's forces—and, for that matter, the strongest White forces—were situated in Ukraine, which was probably the most important theater of the Russian Civil War, as we'll soon see. Denikin was joined by other important White generals, such as Kornilov, as they flew to the Northern Caucasus. There they started to form what was referred to as the Volunteer Army (and the same happened across Russia).

In 1918, the Whites were pushed to their limits and were forced to flee from Rostov to Kuban. This retreat occurred in incredibly harsh winter conditions and is today remembered as the Ice March. Though weakened and heavily outnumbered by the Red Army, the White army, led by Denikin, survived and continued to enlist new recruits. Then came the end of WWI, and the Central Powers were obliged to retreat their forces from all occupied areas, including Ukraine. This produced a "power vacuum" in this region, to be filled with numerous (para)military groups. Initially, the Reds advanced steadily, supported by the Green and Black armies. Then, suddenly, the Greens withdrew their support, and the Reds found themselves unable to repel the attacks of Denikin.

---

[98] The Reds had mastered propaganda, already centralized and firmly under the grip of Lenin long ago.

[99] LEHOVICH, Dimitry V. Denikin's Offensive. *The Russian Review*, 1973, 32.2: 173-186.

Denikin enters Volgograd, then Tsaritsyn.
https://commons.wikimedia.org/w/index.php?curid=8086765

By the summer of 1919, the Whites stationed in Russia's south and in Ukraine had pushed the Reds far up north. For a short while, it looked as if the Whites may take Moscow. However, their troops were overstretched, exhausted, and not-so-well-equipped. In addition, the guerilla forces of another important character in the revolutionary saga, Nestor Makhno, dealt significant blows to the Whites and their southern areas. The majority of White soldiers were pushing for Moscow. In Ukraine, perhaps the most important theater of the Russian Civil War, Makhno was leading his renegade anarchist army against those who he hated the most: royalists, counter-revolutionaries, and reactionaries.

Before we focus on the mass anarchist movement that rose in Ukraine during the civil war, we'll give a brief overview of the downfall of the Whites after the breakdown of their Moscow offensive:

Nestor Makhno's (Black) Army

You may recall that we started this book with early revolutionary attempts and often mentioned Russia's anarchists. In 1918, anarchists, along with other left political groups such as the Left SRs, found themselves increasingly at odds with the Bolsheviks. At the periphery, however, the anarchists implemented their plans in the form of Nestor Makhno's anarchist state (which at one point spread across modern-day southern and eastern Ukraine). On the one hand, Makhno's story is the story of numerous leaders of rebellions across Russia. On the other, it's a very special story of a man who had an interesting vision and an incredibly adventurous life. As his story is very indicative of how life was during the period of civil war in Russia, we'll focus on it a bit more.

Born in a very poor peasant family in 1888, working in fields and factories from a young age, Makhno had what most professional revolutionaries lacked: experience of real, hard work and sympathy for all working people, not simply the urban working class.[100] By the early 20th century, Makhno had accumulated enough experience to join the growing revolutionary movement in his native Ukraine. He joined the Union of Poor Peasants based in his hometown of Huliaipole around 1905 (at sixteen), distributing revolutionary pamphlets. It's at the Union that he learned more about the theoretical bases of revolution, and from this early age Makhno showed propensity for Anarcho-Communism.

Nestor Makhno around 1909.
https://commons.wikimedia.org/w/index.php?curid=33181

However, always more a person of action than of studying, Makhno started participating in peasant actions (organized by the Poor Peasants

---

[100] As mentioned, Lenin was born into a family of intellectuals (who, truth be told, weren't wealthy by any means), and Trotsky was born in a wealthy family. Both received education that only a small proportion of Russian children could expect to receive. Makhno hardly had any school.

Union) aimed at the local wealthy. Groups of militant peasants terrorized wealthy landowners, stealing their property. This brought the Union and Nestor Makhno under the close surveillance of the tsarist police and earned him his long prison sentence in 1909. In fact, Makhno was sentenced to life in prison, where he was supposed to erode his life doing hard labor. After a series of transfers, he ended up in Butyrka prison, which had a large population of political prisoners. There, Nestor Makhno continued the schooling started at the Poor Peasants Union. For instance, he read the works of famous Peter Kropotkin, guided chiefly by a fellow-inmate, Peter Arshinov, another notable anarchist.[101]

Makhno was a man of action even in prison, which earned him long periods of solitary confinement. He was released from prison along with numerous other political prisoners at the onset of the February Revolution. He was now more resolved than ever to take concrete steps to incite peasants to mass action that would end in the establishment of communes working together for mutual benefit. After the February Revolution, there were virtually no hurdles that stopped peasants from confiscating the lands, factories, and workshops that should belong to them. Especially in Huliaipole, far away from Moscow and Petrograd, it was possible to immediately proceed to concrete anarchist organizational activity. The Bolsheviks would soon try to do a similar thing, taking from the rich and giving to the poor, and we know the pitfalls of this redistribution of wealth. Makhno encountered similar difficulties when he was making his Anarcho-Communist heaven. In the words of Victor Peters, one of Makhno's biographers:

"Those who resisted the requisition of their property were beaten, terrorized, or shot, but usually the owners did not resist. This did not necessarily mean they were not beaten and shot, especially if the requisitioners suspected that they had hidden some valuables or money. Still, during the period 1917-1918, relatively few executions took place."[102]

As we can see, the reality of Makhno's dissemination of the anarchic utopia was much grimmer than he himself would be ready to accept.

---

[101] PETERS, Victor. *Nestor Makhno*. Winnipeg: Echo Books, 1971. Available at: https://files.libcom.org/files/Victor_Peters_Makhno.pdf

[102] Ibid. p. 32

And quickly, his dream was under serious threat. In the spring of 1918, German forces, following the Treaty of Brest-Litovsk, invaded Ukraine. The Germans quickly established a puppet regime in Ukraine, led by hetman Skoropadsky.[103] Makhno's anarchist actions were thus quickly counteracted. Expropriated goods were returned to previous owners, and culprits were sometimes punished (e.g., flogged).[104]

Makhno left Ukraine and reached Moscow, where he met the likes of Kropotkin and Lenin. He received reassurances from the Bolsheviks and obtained a forged passport with which he returned to Ukraine to start an insurrection against both the Germans and Ukrainian nationalists. The only type of resistance that was possible, at least initially, was guerilla warfare, and this type of warfare suited Makhno's action-seeking character the best.

Makhno managed to enter Ukraine with his forged passport in the summer of 1918, where he joined the guerilla group of a certain Fedir Shchus, who operated in the Dubrovka Forest near the town of Dubrovka. The authorities learned that something was happening in Dubrovka Forest and decided to encircle the guerilla group and eliminate it once and for all. Makhno and a few followers left the forest to scout the area and learned that enemy forces were stationed in the market square. Returning to the forest, Makhno divided his forces (around thirty men) into two units, the first charged with a flanking attack and the second charging the enemy from the front. This daring attack solidified Makhno's nickname, *batko* (a Ukrainian diminutive for "father"), despite the group having to withdraw due to a serious counterattack.

But Makhno managed to reach his native Huliaipole just in time for the WWI armistice of November 11. In comparison to Brest-Litovsk, it was rather unsatisfactory for the Germans and Austrians, who had to withdraw from all territories they occupied, including Ukraine. Thus, Makhno was free once again to build his anarchic utopia, this time battling the weak Ukrainian nationalists, Whites, Reds, and other military groups. This was the real start of Makhno's Ukrainian Insurgent Army, which started to look more and more like an organized army than

---

[103] Hetman was a traditional Polish-Lithuanian title, also used by Ukrainian Cossacks, a sort of highest military commander.

[104] PETERS, Victor. *Nestor Makhno.* p. 39

a loose guerilla band. Soon, Makhno allied with the Red Army, aiming his attack against the Ukrainian nationalists and the Whites. On occasions, Makhno commanded joint Red-Insurgent forces, for instance in the battle for Katerynoslav (Dnipro) in December 1918, when the town was snatched away from the nationalists.

The ill-fated cooperation between Makhno and the Reds continued into 1919, not without hiccups. Makhno was steadily pursuing his goals, criticizing the Bolshevik regime whenever he found fit. For a few months, the allies maintained a precarious equilibrium, but criticisms aimed at Makhno from high Bolshevik officials became more and more frequent. Some officials, such as Kamenev and Antonov-Ovseenko, even visited the center of Makhno's political and economic actions, Huliaipole, returning to headquarters with words of praise for the great man. However, by mid-1919, the tide had changed, and Makhno started being seen by the Reds more as a threat and an outlaw than an ally. This forced Makhno to enter negotiations with a fellow outlaw and commander of a guerilla Green Army, Nykyfor Hryhoriv, whom we'll soon discuss in detail. For now, let's just say their meeting didn't end well, and the Greens and Makhno parted ways.

Makhno's lieutenants.
https://commons.wikimedia.org/w/index.php?curid=85909068

The animosities between Makhno and the Reds were put on pause, however, as Anton Denikin marched toward Moscow in the summer of

1919. This was perhaps the height of the White's power. After the offensive broke down, the White movement lost its edge and was gradually eradicated from Russia. During this period, the animosities between the Bolsheviks and Makhno were paused. They both focused on fighting the Whites, who expanding their power in Ukraine, advancing towards Moscow from the south of Russia and east Ukraine. (For instance, they took Makhno's Huliaipole, which changed hands rather often during the civil war.) The Reds and Makhno even entered into another alliance, called the Starobilsk agreement, signed in 1920.[105] The agreement was purely a pragmatic one, revolving solely around military matters, with the political struggle left for another time.

With the erosion of the White offensive, the Reds turned against Makhno. And there was no better target than Huliaipole, taken by the Reds in November 1920, only to be recaptured by Makhno soon after.[106] This marked the start of a real rebellion against the Bolsheviks. From then on, Makhno was moving through the fields and forests of Ukraine, trying to inflict as much damage as possible upon the Red forces. Makhno was injured multiple times and had barely escaped the overwhelming Red units on numerous occasions. By July 1921, the anarchist dream was over. Ukraine was under a firm Bolshevik grip, and Makhno was forced into exile, finally settling in Paris with his wife and daughter after much hardship. Exhausted, depressed, suffering from tuberculosis, and increasingly indulging in alcohol, Makhno died in 1934.[107]

The Greens

The title "Greens" was applied to peasant insurgent units operating all around Russia. The most powerful was probably the Green Army of Nykyfor Hryhoriv, who was like Makhno, in the military sense at least.[108] He was likewise a great guerilla commander, but ideologically speaking,

---

[105] MALET, Michael; The End, October 1920-August 1921. *Nestor Makhno in the Russian Civil War*, 1982, 64-80.

[106] As of 2022, Huliaipole is again on the frontline, this time in the war between Ukraine and Russia.

[107] An interesting Russian TV series on Makhno's life is called *Nine Lives of Nestor Makhno*, filmed in 2005.

[108] GILLEY, Christopher. Fighters for Ukrainian independence? Imposture and identity among Ukrainian warlords, 1917-22. *Historical Research*, 2017, 90.247: 172-190.

the two were rather different. Compared to the Bolsheviks and even Makhno, the Green armies didn't have a clear ideology, generally speaking. The Greens were primarily an expression of peasant dissatisfaction with all sides involved in conflict. Practically everyone in the Russian Civil War committed atrocities and crimes, not only the main belligerents—the Reds and Whites—but others, such as Makhno's army. Alas, the Green armies would often commit the same atrocities they despised so much in the Reds, Whites, and other armies.

Nykyfor Hryhoriv was the leader of a large Ukrainian peasant independent movement that gave the Reds some very painful headaches. Initially, Hryhoriv sided with the Ukrainian nationalists and against the Whites. Then, after the downfall of the nationalists, Hryhoriv sided with the Bolsheviks, who had set their foot in Ukraine in early 1919. After helping them deal with their enemies in Ukraine, chiefly the remaining nationalists and Allied interventionists, he turned against the Bolsheviks.[109] Hryhoriv was taken by the White's suppression of the Reds in Ukraine, and probably thought that his was his moment to shine. The Red Army at the time still wasn't that powerful and, during its first offensive in Ukraine in early 1919, relied heavily on Makhno's and Hryhoriv's troops, which wasn't a solution because both armies were disorderly and led by hotheaded, highly autonomous generals.

Hryhoriv, as we already mentioned, was especially unreliable. And, unlike Makhno (who also operated in the south of Ukraine), he didn't have political ideas that would link him to the Bolsheviks (and, for that matter, hardly any coherent political ideas at all). By May 1919, Hryhoriv had completely stopped obeying Bolshevik orders and sought support from Makhno. Makhno himself refused to immediately support the Red Army and preferred to remain neutral towards Hryhoriv.

From then on, events unraveled quickly. Hryhoriv took some areas controlled by the Red Army and was swiftly driven away by a Red counterattack. In June, he was forced to remind Makhno of his previous

---

[109] Russia's allies from WWI supported the White movement and tried to fight the Bolsheviks. The French, for instance, captured Odessa early in 1919, and other cities were captured by the Allies. The UK had forces in Northern Russia, Siberia, and the Caucasus. The Japanese took some Eastern provinces; the Americans had forces in Vladivostok, etc. There was a strong feeling among the Allies that Bolshevism must be suffocated before it got out of hand. Winston Churchill harbored such feelings but, in the end, could only regret the perceived inaction of the Allies.

offer to join forces. But Makhno learned that since Hryhoriv had rebelled, the Red propaganda machine went overboard and criticized not only Hryhoriv but also Makhno by association. Moreover, Makhno's soldiers witnessed numerous crimes committed by Hryhoriv's troops, especially systemic anti-Semitic crimes, which propelled them to plead with Makhno not to side with Hryhoriv.

The two renegade generals met, however, in June 1919. Although it's not completely clear what happened, Hryhoriv didn't get out of this meeting alive. It's likely there was a large meeting where the two leaders held speeches. Makhno openly criticized Hryhoriv for the way he was leading his troops. Then, groups of Hryhoriv's and Makhno's supporters engaged in a sort of Mexican standoff, and Hryhoriv was killed.[110] This scenario is perfectly descriptive of the chaotic environment in civil war Ukraine.

The Resolution of the Russian Civil War

In this section, we'll briefly recapitulate the most important events and battles of the Russian Civil War:

- **Operations in Don and Donbass (early 1918)**: The Soviets pushed the Whites south of Don, resulting in the Ice March. These operations included tens of thousands of soldiers, most of them battling for the Reds, a reoccurring theme throughout the war.
- **Battle of Barnaul (mid-June, 1918)**: The Reds were encircled and pushed out of Barnaul (a Siberian town) by the Whites; around 4,000 soldiers participated in this battle (equally distributed across the two sides).
- **Perm operations (late 1918, early 1919)**: This was another Siberian operation, involving 36,000 Red and 45,000 White soldiers. The outcome of the battle was indecisive, with heavy casualties on both sides.
- **Moscow offensive (summer of 1919): The** Whites, led by Denikin, were initially successful and, at one point, were a few hundred kilometers from Moscow. The inherent problems of the White army (and all armies in the civil war) and Makhno's

---

[110] DARCH, Colin, 2020, Nestor Makhno and Rural Anarchism in Ukraine. *Pluto Press*. Available at: https://diasporiana.org.ua/wp-content/uploads/books/26581/file.pdf

constant attacks behind the backs of the advancing Whites led to the breakdown of the offensive.

- **Voronezh-Kastornoye operation (October/November 1919)**: Through this operation, the Red Army pushed Denikin's forces away from Moscow, practically ending to Moscow offensive.
- **North Caucasus advance of the Red Army (January 1920)**: The Reds managed to push the Whites further south, finally destroying their main strongholds in the North Caucasus. This precipitated a chaotic evacuation of Novorossiysk in early spring of 1920.Thousands of White troops were captured as they failed to evacuate to Crimea.

Chapter 8: A "New Economic Policy" – Russia After the Revolution

Faced with the terrible famine of 1921 and 1922, raging inflation, and ever more serious and organized revolts (e.g., the Tambov rebellion of 1920, quenched in 1922, alongside the Krondstadt rebellion of Red sailors instrumental in the revolutionary success of the Bolsheviks), Lenin was forced to introduce a new economic plan: the New Economic Policy (NEP).[111, 112]

Introduced in 1921, the NEP was a belated but ultimately successful response to the USSR's difficulties, putting end to years of War Communism.[113] Lenin realized that the time wasn't right to enforce radical Marxism. Previously-banned free market and private enterprises were reinstated. (Needless to say, large industries and financial sector remained firmly in the grip of the Communists.) Moreover, the concept of profit was reintroduced even to state-owned companies. Most

---

[111] WEISSMAN, Benjamin M. *Herbert Hoover and Famine Relief to Soviet Russia, 1921-1923.* Hoover Institution Press, 1974.

[112] POLLACK, Emanuel. *The Kronstadt Rebellion: The First Armed Revolt Against the Soviets.* Philosophical Library, 1959.

[113] RICHMAN, Sheldon L. War Communism to NEP: the road from serfdom. *The Journal of Libertarian Studies*, 1981, 5.1: 89-97.

importantly, the NEP oversaw a cease in forced requisitions of grain and instead introduced a "food tax."

A bustling market, NEP period.
https://commons.wikimedia.org/w/index.php?curid=31424079

The economic landscape of revolutionary Russia was abysmal, to say the least. Inflation was increasing even before the February and October revolutions, a heritage from the breakdown of the old tsarist regime. The civil war dealt a final blow to the Russian economy. During this period, money literally became valueless. By 1921, as the civil war raged on, the total economic output of the country decreased to just a fraction of what it had been just a few years prior. The deadly spiral of inflation, spurred by the winds of the Bolshevik revolution and especially their grand War Communism project, practically brought the country's economy to a halt. With prices skyrocketing due to a general lack of all essential goods, the Bolsheviks resorted to printing more money, quickly succeeding in destroying the ruble.

Hyperinflation

In 1919, rising inflation became hyperinflation when the Bolsheviks allowed the People's Bank to print limitless amounts of money to cover government expenses.[114] The budget deficit was "filled" by simply

---

[114] PICKERSGILL, Joyce E. Hyperinflation and Monetary Reform in the Soviet Union, 1921-26. *Journal of Political Economy*, 1968, 76.5: 1037-1048.

printing more money. Since the Bolsheviks refused to take on the foreign debts of the previous government, they couldn't get any foreign loans. Moreover, War Communism attempted to completely abolish all currencies, as the Bolsheviks were convinced that a modern economy could function without money. It can be hard to imagine the sheer lack of competence, coupled with an absolute disregard for finance and the economy, shared by most Bolsheviks. Here's what Nicholas Krestinski, Commissar of Finance (the Bolshevik version of a minister of finance), had to say in 1919 as the hyperinflation set its foot in Soviet Russia:

"Finance should not exist in a socialistic community and I must, therefore, apologize for speaking on the subject."[115] Budget planning, and for that matter, proper budget expenditure estimates, were virtually impossible, and the Commissariat of Finance resorted to a tragicomic measure, issuing *retrospective* budget plans.

Barter was an attempt to save the Russian economy during the crescendo of the Civil War. In fact, the peasants were already resorting to barter because the currencies were unstable and becoming increasingly valueless. The Bolsheviks started to believe they could completely stop using money and build their whole economy on barter. Like most things related to War Communism, barter was planned centrally. Lenin focused on this issue and, by May 1921, was advocating for its importance and more widespread application throughout the Soviet economy.[116] The Bolsheviks were mostly channeling industrial goods toward the villages to obtain grain. The initial results were interpreted as unsatisfactory, as local Soviets often failed to obtain a fair deal with the peasants and constantly undersupplied grain. In fact, the Bolsheviks only procured 4.5 percent of the expected quantity.[117]

The barter experiment was quickly deemed a failure by most Bolsheviks, including Lenin. However, bartering cleared the land and provided a transition to the New Economic Policy, which ultimately got the Soviet Union out of the inflation spiral. The failure of centrally-planned barter further propelled hyperinflation, stalling the transition to

---

[115] EFREMOV, Steven M. *The role of inflation in soviet history: Prices, living standards, and political change.* 2012. PhD Thesis. East Tennessee State University.

[116] SOKOLOV, N. G. The Use of Barter During the Transition to NEP. *Soviet Studies in History*, 1984, 23.2: 54-61.

[117] Ibid. p. 59

the only real solution, which was gold-backed currency.

Numerous post-WWI countries were engulfed in hyperinflation: Germany (Weimar Republic), Hungary, Poland, and Austria were all in a very similar situation as the Soviets: "(...) all of the countries were facing the consequences of excessive wartime spending, large government budget deficits, physical destruction, output collapse, territorial and population loss. Because of the economic and budgetary problems, the governments of these countries resorted to issuing ever-increasing amounts of unbacked paper money to finance their expenditures. Invariably, these policies caused hyperinflation and economic chaos."[118]

Starting in 1922, chervonets, a gold-backed currency, were introduced in what had by this time become the gigantic Soviet Union.[119, 120] By 1924, as the NEP unraveled, hyperinflation was finally put under control. On January 21, 1924, Vladimir Ilyich Ulyanov, nicknamed Lenin, died, possibly due to injuries sustained in 1918 when Fanny Kaplan tried to kill him.[121] Lenin was the *de facto* supreme ruler of USSR until his death, a lifelong Chairman of the Council of People's Commissars of the Soviet Union. This was perhaps one of the reasons the succession issue was left largely unresolved. In the end, Lenin was cremated and his body was put on display in Moscow's Red Square.[122]

---

[118] EFREMOV, Steven M. *The role of inflation in soviet history: Prices, living standards, and political change.* 2012. PhD Thesis. East Tennessee State University.

[119] BARNETT, Vincent. As Good as Gold? A Note on the chervonets. *Europe-Asia Studies*, 1994, 46.4: 663-669.

[120] The formal proclamation of the Union of Soviet Socialist Republics (USSR) was made in December 28, 1922. By the end of 1922, the Bolsheviks had finally quenched all opposing forces in their country, installing Communist regimes across all countries that were once part of the Russian Empire but now flirted with independence.

[121] Lenin suffered a series of strokes prior to his death and, for the previous three or four years, was in very bad shape. This might be one of the reasons Stalin could consolidate his power and prepare for his great onslaught after Lenin died.

[122] This is an incredibly ironic end of a man who was a devout atheist. It's likely that both Lenin's wishes and the wishes of his family were much humbler and more in accordance with their beliefs.

The end of the NEP and Rise of Stalinism

Thanks to policies that encouraged entrepreneurship and private enterprise, the NEP gave birth to a new class: the so-called "NEPmen."[123] These were a few million people who made their fortune thanks to looser economic policies. Craftsmen, peasants, urban workers, and experts, were all given opportunity to put their products on a relatively free market. The NEP, much like the barter experiment, was of course anti-Communist and was regarded as a transitory concession to the gravity of the situation.

Here's an example of what the NEP improved: peasants could sell their grain and pay taxes in money. This sounds rather basic, but it's an incredible improvement compared to forced grain requisitions. Motivated to produce more grain so they could sell more, peasants increased the output, and this (at least for a while) distanced fears about the next big famine.[124] Soviet agriculture, slowly but surely, surpassed the agricultural output of pre-revolutionary years. As there was more grain, its price tended to fall. NEP-motivated middle men were buying grain from peasants and trying to resell it at higher prices.

The Bolsheviks had mixed feelings about the NEPmen: on the one hand, their existence was deemed necessary, at least for a while. But there were many Bolsheviks who denounced the utterly capitalist and bourgeois NEPmen. Although the NEP solved the most urgent issues in the newly-born USSR, it postponed the implementation of essential Leninist ideas, such as collectivization. From the outset, it was clear that the NEP wouldn't last forever and that, sooner or later, the USSR will revert to hardcore Marxist policies. It was up to Lenin's successors to solve this issue and ensure a smooth transition to real Communism.

---

[123] BALL, Alan M. *Russia's last capitalists: the Nepmen, 1921-1929*. Univ of California Press, 1990.

[124] You may recall that we already discussed the Russian famine of 1921-1922, when millions of people died of hunger.

Chapter 9: Stalinism: The Real Legacy of the Russian Revolution

Ioseb Besarionis Dzhugashvili, later known as Stalin (literally "man of steel"), stepped to the forefront as Lenin succumbed to illness.[125] Stalin's rise wasn't haphazard. For decades, Stalin had been an able, active, and implacable Bolshevik. But let's look further down the road of the past into Stalin's early childhood, as it's here we can find (potential and partial) explanations for some of the worst things that beset the USSR.

Young Ioseb.
https://commons.wikimedia.org/w/index.php?curid=96948659

---

[125]Often written as "Joseph Vissarionovich."

Ioseb Dzhugashvili, born on December 18, 1878, was the only child of his mother, Ekaterine Geladze and Besarion Dzhugashvili, as his brothers and sisters all died in infancy. The family lived in a Georgian town called Gori, at the time an integral part of the Russian Empire. Stalin's mother and father soon parted ways after Besarion lost his job in a cobbler workshop, indulged in alcohol, and started beating his wife and son. Stalin then embarked on an arduous and traumatic journey with his mother, moving across Georgia for years and changing residences numerous times.[126]

Finally, thanks to a family friend (who was a priest), Stalin was accepted into an Orthodox Church school. Like many other revolutionaries, Stalin excelled in school and was eventually accepted into Orthodox Theological University in Tiflis (another Georgian town).[127] Stalin's interest for religion, however, dwindled, and he became interested in forbidden literature. Chernyshevsky's *What Is to Be Done?* (published in 1863), which openly attacked the Russian monarchy and boldly tackled the question of removing tsar from power, served as a major inspiration to Stalin, as well as most other revolutionaries. (It is said that both Nechayev and Lenin all held *What Is to Be Done?* in high regards.)

Stalin quickly devoured socialist and Marxist literature, establishing connections with likeminded Georgians, and was recognized as a threat by the Okhrana around 1900. Stalin was thriving in the pre-revolutionary atmosphere of the Russian Empire, incessantly calling workers to protests and strikes and writing inflammatory slogans and pamphlets. From then on, Stalin lived the life of a fugitive, going from one hiding spot to another and being supported by fellow Marxists. Stalin then found work in a factory in Batum (an important port city in Georgia), hoping that this position would help him to inspire workers to act. His provocations earned him a prison sentence and a ticket to exile in 1902. However, in 1904, Stalin escaped and returned from Siberian exile to Georgia. From then on, Stalin's actions radicalized, and the man started organizing a sort of Bolshevik paramilitary unit, which started operating in the chaos of the 1905 revolution in Georgia.

---

[126] CORBESERO, Susan. History, Myth, and Memory: A Biography of a Stalin Portrait. *Russian History*, 2011, 38.1: 58-84.

[127] Stalin also wrote good poetry, often with romantic and poignant overtones.

Stalin in 1902, picture taken by the police.
https://commons.wikimedia.org/w/index.php?curid=211215

 These squads commanded by Stalin functioned like a mafia: their primary goal was to obtain money for the party, and almost any action was justified—racketeering, heists, robberies, etc. One of the most daring and successful actions taken by the Bolshevik mafia was the robbery of the Tiflis bank in 1907, organized primarily by Stalin. Preparations for the robbery were substantial: Stalin procured info from inside men and knew that on June 26, 1907, a large sum of money would be brought to the bank.[128]

 The gang was well-organized, supplied with weapons and bombs, and disguised in peasant clothes. They were everywhere around the bank, also lurking from a nearby tavern. The signal being given, the robbers quickly overwhelmed the guards surrounding the carriage that carried the money to the bank. They had their own carriage, a quick phaeton, used to transport the stolen money to their headquarters. The rider of this phaeton, a certain Kamo, was disguised as a military officer and only narrowly avoided soldiers who, a few blocks away, wanted to search him.

---

[128] READ, Christopher. *Stalin: From the Caucasus to the Kremlin.* Taylor & Francis, 2016.

This is just one example of the type of crimes committed by Stalin's gang. The group quickly moved to Baku, where it continued with robberies, kidnappings (usually children of rich people), and racketeering. These actions led to a new prison sentence, this time in Baku (1908), and later exile to Vologda province (1909). The sheer incapability of the tsarist prison system again became obvious as Stalin again escaped exile and went to Petrograd, only to be quickly recaptured and sent back to Vologda in 1910. In 1911, he escaped yet again and was sent for the third time to Vologda. In 1912, Stalin became a member of the Central Committee, owing to his lack of scruples and ability to procure money for the party. The same year, he became the editor of *Pravda* (literally "justice"), the all-important Bolshevik-run newspaper.

Another mug shot of Stalin. This one contains personal info.
https://commons.wikimedia.org/w/index.php?curid=1844719

After a few more arrests and escapes, Stalin traveled abroad to visit Lenin in late 1912 and early 1913. There, with Lenin's guidance, Stalin started writing one of his most important essays, *Marxism and the National Question.*[129] This is a rigorous, dry text purporting to answer

---

[129] Available at: https://archive.org/details/marxismnationalquestion/page/n7/mode/2up

essential questions concerning what a nation is, and most importantly, the role of nationality in Marxism. In it, Stalin enumerates all the defining characteristics of a nation: a common language, common territory, and common psychological character. He moves on to conclude:

"A nation is a historically constituted, stable community of people, formed on the basis of a common language, territory, economic life, and psychological make-up manifested in a common culture."[130]

Stalin, who would soon use the whole USSR as his playfield, forcibly moving entire ethnic groups—millions of people—from one end of his empire to another, in this article argues *for,* not against, the right of self-determination. He says: "(...) Marxists cannot dispense with the right of nations to self-determination."[131] What permeates the whole article, however, is not a lullaby to the right of self-determination but a dismantling of the concept of nationality. In Stalin's opinion, and generally speaking within Marxism-Leninism, a nation is an artificial creation, bound together by sheer necessity. Moreover, nationality itself is a shaky concept, as there is not a single defining characteristic of a nation. Stalin concludes the article with a somewhat more typical Stalinist quote: "There is no middle course: principles triumph, they do not 'compromise.'"[132] Together with his general deprecation of nationalism, this quote implicitly announces Stalin's future large-scale social experiments: the destruction of whole nations via forced relocations, all in the name of unification under the flag of Communism.

This article shows that Stalin was an astute observer of the world and a good intellectual worker, akin to Lenin.[133] *Marxism and the National Question* cemented Stalin's reputation among the higher circles of Bolsheviks.

Returning from Cracow where he had met Lenin, Stalin was arrested yet again in February 1913. This time, Stalin was sent thousands of miles east to Siberia, to Turukhansk. As was customary for him over the course of his numerous exiles, Stalin spent time searching for new

---

[130]STALIN, Joseph. *Marxism and the National Question Internet* Archive; p. 16

[131]Ibid. p. 100

[132]Ibid. p. 108

[133]Stalin's bitter enemy, Trotsky, questioned Stalin's authorship of this article.

romantic interests. The Turukhansk exile was his longest one, as escape was virtually impossible, and it's where Stalin spent the first few years of WWI. Stalin almost got conscripted into the Russian Imperial Army in 1916 but was ultimately rejected due to having a deformed and dysfunctional left arm (due to a childhood injury). After a few more months of exile idleness came the February Revolution, and Stalin returned triumphantly to Petrograd and resumed his work as *Pravda* editor.

Instrumental over the course of the ensuing Bolshevik Revolution, Stalin saw a lot of action. As a *Pravda* editor, he witnessed firsthand (and had to escape from) the clampdown of Provisionals and their raids of Bolshevik propaganda centers. He also had a major role in ensuring Lenin's safety and that he wasn't arrested by the Provisionals. Later, as the civil war was raging, Stalin became a military commander.[134]

Toward Dictatorship: Stalin's Rise

We've seen how Stalin slowly made his way to the top: becoming a prominent figure of Georgian revolutionary movement, organizing paramilitary formations, and procuring money for the Bolsheviks. Stalin became an indispensable assistant to Lenin.

Lenin's declining health in the last few years of his life, starting in 1921, confined his movements and made him dependent on people like Stalin. Stalin was the quickest to understand what needed to be done: a major political offensive, disguised as Lenin's closest assistant. In 1922, Stalin became the General Secretary (appointed by Lenin) of the Communist Party, a position he would keep until his death in 1953.[135] Perhaps Lenin was hoping to have someone he could trust as a general secretary, someone stern and able, while he was recovering. Although seriously ill, even in late 1922, he could correctly predict the future: that is, the rift between Stalin and Trotsky, as well as the dangers that lay

---

[134] Stalin was a ruthless "general" (like most other Bolshevik military commanders, Stalin had little military training or knowledge) and was even reprimanded by his comrades for his propensity for harsh punitive measures and recklessness. Stalin had little regard for his troops, and often his orders resulted in numerous men being killed needlessly. It's not surprising that once Stalin became the Red Tsar, and WWII raged throughout Europe, he employed his methods on an epochal scale.

[135] BROWN, Archie. The Power of the General Secretary of the CPSU. *Authority, power and policy in the USSR: Essays Dedicated to Leonard Schapiro*, 1983, 135-157.

behind Stalin's appointment as General Secretary of the Communist Party:

"I think that from this standpoint the prime factors in the question of stability are such members of the C.C. as Stalin and Trotsky. I think relations between them make up the greater part of the danger of a split, which could be avoided, and this purpose, in my opinion, would be served, among other things, by increasing the number of C.C. members to 50 or 100.

Comrade Stalin, having become Secretary-General, has unlimited authority concentrated in his hands, and I am not sure whether he will always be capable of using that authority with sufficient caution. Comrade Trotsky, on the other hand, as his struggle against the C.C. on the question of the People's Commissariat of Communications has already proved, is distinguished not only by outstanding ability. He is personally perhaps the most capable man in the present C.C., but he has displayed excessive self-assurance and shown excessive preoccupation with the purely administrative side of the work."[136]

Lenin and Stalin in 1922.
https://commons.wikimedia.org/w/index.php?curid=6903456

---

[136] LENIN, Vladimir Ilich Ulyanov. Letters to the Congress. Available at: https://www.marxists.org/archive/lenin/works/1922/dec/testamnt/congress.htm

Lenin's assessment of Stalin as "crude," "capricious," and "intolerant," were all correct. In early January 1923, Lenin advised his comrades to remove Stalin from the top of the Communist Party. However, once in power, Stalin knew how to remain in power, appointing his most servile supporters to important posts. Moreover, he knew when to strike: he didn't try to take all power by force; he was ready to wait for years.

His biggest opponent, of course, was Trotsky, who according to Lenin, was a somewhat more able politician. Trotsky, of course, personified the Bolshevik victory in the civil war and was a Red Army man through-and-through. Trotsky also held an important post as the People's Commissar for Military and Naval Affairs of the Soviet Union. Perhaps knowing that he essentially had the whole Soviet military might under his command, Trotsky refused Lenin's offer to become the Chairman of the Council of People's Commissars in 1922, which had been Lenin's position since 1917. To numerous people, this was a sign that Lenin designated Trotsky as his "successor." The refusal was a big mistake, as Trotsky's influence in USSR politics steadily decreased from then on, especially after Lenin's death.

Meanwhile, Stalin sided with Kamenev and Zinoviev, obtaining their support in his fight against Trotsky at least for a while.[137, 138] Trotsky, attempting to retain a semblance of free speech within the Communist Party, denounced the increasing bureaucratization headed by Stalin, which further cemented Trotsky's position as *persona non grata*. Trotsky further made things worse for himself because he opposed the NEP, heading the Left Opposition, which wanted a return to the real Bolshevik economic policies.

By 1925, Trotsky lost his position as the head of Red Army, with numerous comrades denouncing him as anti-Bolshevik and a bourgeois.

---

[137] Grigory Zinoviev was Chairman of the Communist International and Chairman of the Petrograd Soviet, while Lev Kamenev was Deputy Chairman of the Council of People's Commissars and head of the Lenin Institute. The ability to ally with important Bolsheviks (even though most of them didn't share his views) was key to his rise to power. Stalin knew how to placate people and coax them into supporting him. Moreover, and perhaps even more importantly, Stalin always had the secret Soviet police (the Cheka and then NKVD) firmly under his command.

[138] O'CONNOR, Timothy Edward. *Stalin and Trotsky 1926-1928*. PhD Thesis. Graduate School. P. 24

These denouncements were sometimes so fierce and emotional that they left human casualties. For instance, Felix Dzerzhinsky, the head of the infamous Cheka, died of a heart attack in 1926, hours after delivering a fiery speech against Trotsky.

Stalin was determined to expel all those who questioned his authority and cancel their Communist Party membership. This is exactly what happened to Trotsky, who continued to disagree. After being exiled to Kazakhstan and then deported to Turkey in 1929, Trotsky realized his dream of the permanent revolution was finally and decidedly over—and so was any semblance of free speech in Soviet Union.

Stalin's Policies
Five-Year Planning and Shift Back to Radical Communism

Stalin's support for the NEP was calculated: he knew that if he expressed his disagreement with Lenin's policies too early, it could have been detrimental to his reputation. So, he worked to establish a solid power base. By 1928, with most political opponents (like Trotsky) sidelined or deported, Stalin put an end to the NEP, reverting to something much more like War Communism.

Here's what Mr. Knickerbocker, who personally visited the USSR during the First Five Year Plan, had to say about it:

"Some of the specific objectives are to double power, oil, coal and steel production; to triple metal production; to quadruple machine production, all in the course of five years; in short, to multiply at least by two the total output of all industry and to collectivise all farms."[139]

---

[139] KNICKERBOCKER, H. R. The Soviet Five-Year Plan. *International Affairs (Royal Institute of International Affairs 1931-1939)*, 1931, 10.4: 433-459. P. 434

First Five Year Plan propaganda poster; nicely shows how Communists were eager to change even the unbeatable logic of arithmetic.
https://commons.wikimedia.org/w/index.php?curid=54951920

The pendulum was now hurling toward the other extreme, the total opposite of the NEP. The USSR was back to complete central planning of the economy, no free trade, no enterprises, no entrepreneurs—only gigantic state-owned industrial centers and collectivized agriculture. The NEP was a big concession to peasants, who, for a short while, could work their land in peace. The First Five Year Plan brought this to an end, as peasants once again could only look as their land, products, and animals, were taken from them. And so, the Soviet secret police was once again engaged in forceful requisitions of grain.

The first Five Year Plan was an attempt to quickly catch up with the global leading powers, such as the US, France, and the UK. The USSR would, in a few short years, cover a developmental path that realistically could only be completed in decades. Overly optimistic and authoritarian leaders wanted, for instance, to transform Nizhny-Novgorod into an automobile-producing behemoth, planning to produce more than 100,000 cars per year. According to Mr. Knickerbocker, at the time, the

USSR didn't even have 100,000 cars in utilization.[140]

It is, however, easy to underestimate the power generated by the first Five Year Plan. Even a very skeptical observer such as Mr. Knickerbocker had to concede:

"Figures such as these sound fantastic. In Moscow it is easy to dismiss them as Soviet statistics or Soviet dreams. In Azbest they were easy to believe. A day spent in a tour of the mines almost forces conviction: 13,000 men working in seven-hour shifts the clock around are mining 10,000 tons of rock a day. Chasms like Western American canyons sink deep into the ground, and in their depths steam shovels dig mountainous mouthfuls."[141]

But there were millions of deaths due to this First Five Year Plan (and later Five Year Plans). The most appalling consequence was most certainly Holodomor. In 1932 and 1933, the consequences of forced industrialization and collectivization, coupled with a year of bad harvests, couldn't be hidden: up to five million people in Ukraine died of hunger. Millions more died across the USSR.

Purges

Show trials, accusations without any evidence, and executions of political enemies had already been a thing for some time when Stalin decided to step up the game. The Shakhty Trial is one such example. In 1928, a group of engineers were accused of damaging the state thanks to their reckless actions. Previously, there had been at least some logic to sentencing immediate political enemies such as Left Socialist-Revolutionaries. But there was hardly any logic to sentencing and executing dozens of engineers working on the periphery of the USSR (and, for that matter, probably working hard to make the grandiose first Five Year Plan happen).

It's possible the accused weren't devoted Bolsheviks or did not agree with the government on how the grand Five Year Plan should be materialized. But they most certainly weren't counterrevolutionaries who somehow aimed to sabotage the government. Nevertheless, the engineers were executed—people like Peter Palchinsky and Nicholas von

---

[140] It is ironic and entirely anti-Bolshevik that one of the principal investors in this plant was Henry Ford.

[141] KNICKERBOCKER, H. R. The Soviet Five-Year Plan. P. 439

Meck, expert engineers who contributed to the development of mining and railways in the USSR.[142]

From then on, show trials multiplied. In 1930, intellectuals once again found themselves targeted by the government. Some were executed, while others were sent to the Gulag. Among those imprisoned was Leonid Ramzin, a leading Soviet thermal engineer. In an incredible turn of fate typical of Stalinist purges, Leonid Ramzin was released from the Gulag and allowed to continue working on his inventions, while Nicholas Krylenko, the lead prosecutor of the case, was shot in 1938 as part of the Great Purge.

Stalinist purges quickly became more generalized, more violent, and even more chaotic. Anyone could be targeted: high Soviet officials, scientists, intellectuals, working-class people, and peasants. As the Stalinist paranoia grew, it needed more and more victims, and it didn't matter who the victims were. Those who weren't executed were sent to Gulags, where they spent years in horrible circumstances, lacking even basic necessities such as food and warm shelter. The most notorious Gulags were those situated in Russia's far north, where prisoners literally froze to death or died of malnourishment and disease. Indeed, the Gulags were used as a way to punish people for their (presumed) disobedience.[143]

The Great Purge, starting from about 1936, saw a full development of Stalinist paranoia. The old revolutionaries were executed: for the most part, people like Zinoviev, Kamenev, and less important Bolsheviks such as Karl Radek and Yuri Pyatakov. It seems the regime was very focused on obtaining confessions, and by any means possible. Torture, chronic sleep deprivation, and promises that family members would be spared

---

[142] The infamous Article 58 of Soviet Penal Code was used prominently for this show trial. "Improved" and "refined" over years, Article 58 became so vague, abstract, and general that it could be applied to practically any activity (allegedly it was used to stop counterrevolutionary activity). Millions of normal, everyday people were sent to Gulag as "political prisoners" thanks to Article 58.

[143] Mass purges also provided a free workforce, indispensable to the precarious Soviet economy. Millions of people toiled away their lives in the massive Gulag system built under Stalin's careful eye. Gulag prisoners, for instance, dug Belomorkanal between 1931 and 1933. This colossal project connected Petrograd (then Leningrad) and the White Sea. Possibly more than 100,000 people worked on this canal, all from the Gulag system, and likely tens of thousands of people died during its construction.

were just some of the means of forcing a confession.

But top officials were only a small proportion of the people who died during the Great Purge. It's likely that hundreds of thousands of people were executed in the two years of the Great Purge, and hundreds of thousands were sent to Gulags. Millions more would perish in new purges, and these would end only with Stalin's death in 1953.

Vinnytsia massacre perpetrated by the NKVD in 1937-1938.
https://commons.wikimedia.org/w/index.php?curid=3119574

A Gulag mine in Kolyma in the far east of Russia in Russia's Arctic Circle.
The original uploader was Oxonhutch at English Wikipedia. - Transferred from en.wikipedia to Commons., CC BY 2.5, https://commons.wikimedia.org/w/index.php?curid=2121204

Forced labor in Kolyma.
https://commons.wikimedia.org/w/index.php?curid=1302801

Chapter 10: Key Figures of the Russian Revolution

So far, we talked about numerous people important for revolution in one way or another. Many other important personalities deserve to be mentioned, and in this section, we'll briefly focus on these individuals:

- Rasputin
- Lev Kamenev
- Grigory Zinoviev
- Yakov Sverdlov
- Alexandra Kollontai

Grigori Rasputin

Rasputin is one of those people who prosper on others' ignorance, fear, and suffering. He was born in 1869 in the Tobolsk region (Siberia), but the early phases of his life are veiled in mystery. In 1897, he started traveling Russia as a pilgrim, visiting some of the numerous holy places across the country.

In the 1900s, Rasputin already had his famous appearance, mannerisms, and charisma. He was held in high regard by communities of those who believed Rasputin was a very wise man and could help people improve their lives.

The Russian aristocracy of the period was very interested in the esoteric and spiritual and already used the services of mystics and healers such as Nizier Anthelme Philippe and Gérard Encausse. Rasputin fit nicely into this atmosphere and was becoming popular among the aristocracy. By 1905, he met Nicholas II Romanov and Alexandra. Their only son, Alexei Nikolaevich, suffered from hemophilia, and the family increasingly relied on Rasputin to treat their son's condition. Very quickly, and especially in periods when Alexei's condition seemed to worsen, Rasputin became the royal family's closest friend and healer. Alexandra and her confidantes were convinced that Rasputin had supernatural powers that allowed him to heal people.[144]

Rasputin with the royal family in 1908.
https://commons.wikimedia.org/w/index.php?curid=10863452

---

[144] Rasputin was often contacted when Alexei's condition worsened, and it seemed that whenever Rasputin prayed or performed healing rituals, Alexei would get better. Sometimes even professional doctors couldn't explain why Alexei got better. Rasputin was skeptical about modern medicine and may have advised the family not to give any kind of medicine to Alexei, including aspirin, an anti-coagulant. (This wasn't known at the time, however.) This may have helped improve Alexei's health.

Rasputin, however, quickly gained numerous enemies in the highest circles of Russian society. He was accused of heresy by church officials and despised by the Duma due to his alleged influence on the royal family. Many people wanted Rasputin dead. Moreover, denouncements of Rasputin's indecent sexual behavior were becoming more and more frequent. In 1914, an ex-follower, Khioniya Guseva, attempted to kill Rasputin, wounding him severely with a knife.

In 1916, another assassination attempt was made, this time successful. Members of the nobility, led by Grand Duke Dmitri Pavlovich and Prince Felix Yusupov, conspired to kill Rasputin as they saw him as a major threat to the Russian state. Luring him into what seemed to be a party, they first tried to poison him by making him eat cakes and drink wine laced with cyanide. Rasputin didn't seem to be affected by these, so the conspirators decided to shoot him. Yusupov shot Rasputin in the chest, and he fell as if dead. Yusupov went out of the room and came back in, only to be attacked by a very much alive Rasputin. Rasputin was then shot several more times and finally thrown into Malaya Nevka River.

Lev Kamenev and Grigory Zinoviev

We've mentioned Kamenev and Zinoviev but not in detail. Kamenev's real name was Lev Borisovich Rosenfeld, and he was born in a well-off family who could support his education from early life. Kamenev's father had Jewish heritage but was, like many Jewish people in the Russian Empire, a convert to Orthodox Christianity. The fact that Kamenev, like many other Bolsheviks (e.g., Trotsky, born as Lev Bronstein; Grigory Zinoviev, born as Ovsei-Gershon Aronovich Radomyslsky; Yakov Sverdlov, and many others) was Jewish fueled counterrevolutionary paranoia and fed White propaganda, which saw in Bolshevism another devious Jewish plot to rule the world.

Grigory Zinoviev was also born in a well-off Jewish family in 1883 on the periphery of the Russian Empire. Schooled at home, Zinoviev quickly showed an intellectual gift and started reading philosophy, including works on Marxism. He joined the Bolshevik ranks and became one of Lenin's most important associates.

Encountering revolutionary ideas in his nuclear family, young Kamenev quickly became a devout revolutionary himself. He was the more intellectual type of Bolshevik and much more moderate compared to numerous other Bolsheviks. The same was true for Zinoviev. Very early on, Kamenev advocated a more conciliatory relationship between the Bolsheviks and Provisionals. When the Bolsheviks voted for or against organizing an armed revolt against the Provisionals, Kamenev and Zinoviev were the only ones to vote against.

They continued expressing their indignation with militarization in detriment of democracy, resigning from their Central Committee roles. However, they soon returned, Kamenev becoming a sort of deputy to Lenin before the latter's death. From then on, Kamenev and Zinoviev vacillated between supporting Stalin and his opposition, never settling for either. Kamenev and Zinoviev teamed up with Stalin to oust Trotsky. This was a very unlikely alliance, especially considering Kamenev and Zinoviev's previous status as moderate Bolsheviks. Kamenev, moreover, had a familial connection to Trotsky, who married Kamenev's sister Olga.[145]

We can only speculate about the fate of the USSR had Zinoviev and Kamenev sided with Trotsky. It's likely they underestimated Stalin's capacity and ambition, helping him retain his crucial position as the head of the Communist Party. Perhaps they feared more the obviously ambitious and self-confident Trotsky, who spared no one and rarely hesitated to speak what he deemed as truth. Once the animosities began, the situation was further perpetrated when Trotsky published his October Revolution memoires in which he described Kamenev's and Zinoviev's reticence during the days of turmoil.

After this, the infamous troika of Kamenev, Zinoviev, and Stalin seriously damaged Trotsky's position in the Communist Party and removed him from his essential Red Army duties in 1925. We believe this was the turning point for the USSR. Until this moment, Stalin was fairly moderate or, better put, cautious. Once Trotsky was removed from the picture, the troika collapsed, lacking a common enemy. When Kamenev and Zinoviev tried to oust Stalin, it was already too late: the "Steel Man" received support from other important Bolsheviks, such as Nicholas Bukharin and Alexei Rykov. Once again, they were removed from their positions and expelled from the Communist Party, alongside Trotsky. While Trotsky never stopped criticizing Stalin, Bukharin and Zinoviev backed down and were readmitted to the Communist

---

[145] ANFERTIEV, Ivan A. LD Trotsky, GE Zinoviev, and LB Kamenev: the Failed Successors to VI Lenin. *RSUH/RGGU Bulletin: "Literary Theory. Linguistics. Cultural Studies" Series*, 2018, 5: 37-48.

bureaucracy, though this time they had much lower positions.

This was perhaps the most pitiful period of both Kamenev and Zinoviev's lives: unable to speak their minds anymore, they had to apologize for their previous behavior and silently follow the Stalinist line. But this wasn't enough for Stalin. As the Great Purge commenced, Kamenev and Zinoviev found themselves accused of organizing a counterrevolutionary group and were executed in 1936. Their families were also persecuted, sent to Gulags, and some of the members executed.[146]

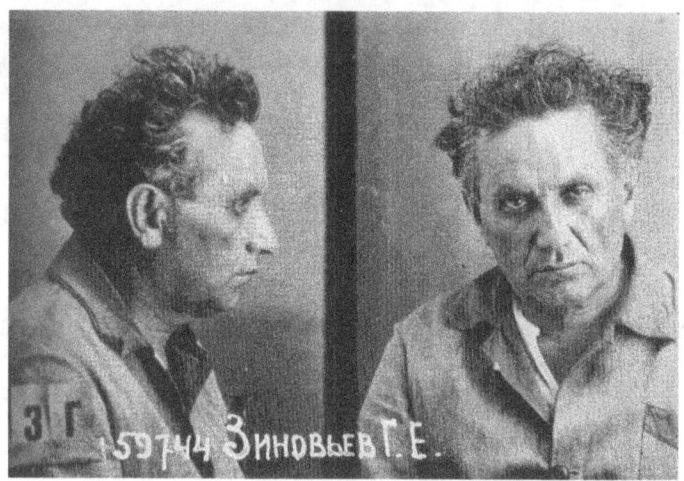

Zinoviev's NKVD mugshot, taken shortly before his execution.
https://commons.wikimedia.org/w/index.php?curid=19314591

Lev Kamenev in 1920s.
https://commons.wikimedia.org/w/index.php?curid=122357294

---

[146] HUTLEY, F. C. The Moscow Trials. *The Australian Quarterly*, 1937, 9.2: 77-86.

Yakov Sverdlov

Yakov Sverdlov is another typical Bolshevik intellectual, born into a middle-class Jewish family in 1885. Sverdlov's father was an active revolutionary, helping forge official documents. Growing up in this kind of environment, Sverdlov quickly became a revolutionary, and after finishing gymnasium as an excellent student, became involved in the actions of nascent Bolsheviks.

Spending a lot of time in imperial prisons and in exile, Sverdlov returned to the capital once the February Revolution started to unravel. A major part of his exile was spent together with Stalin, and the two weren't exactly best friends. Sverdlov's intellectual demeanor and interests didn't sit well with cruder Stalin. There are even some reports that Sverdlov was disgusted by Stalin's hygiene: the latter, for instance, didn't want to wash the dishes but would rather leave it to his dog to lick them.[147]

Sverdlov was known as the party's organizer and even received praise as such by none other than Stalin.[148] Lenin probably intended to have Sverdlov as the first General Secretary of the Communist Party. Unfortunately for Sverdlov, he didn't survive the great Spanish flu pandemic, succumbing to this disease in 1919.

Yakov Sverdlov around 1919.
https://commons.wikimedia.org/w/index.php?curid=69276823

---

[147] GESEEN, Keith. How Stalin Became Stalinist. *The New Yorker*. 2017; https://www.newyorker.com/magazine/2017/11/06/how-stalin-became-stalinist

[148] STALIN, J.V. Y.M. Sverdlov. Available at: https://www.marxists.org/reference/archive/stalin/works/1924/11/x01.htm

Alexandra Kollontai

Alexandra (born Alexandra Mikhailovna Domontovich) was an important Bolshevik born in 1872 into a wealthy Ukrainian family. Excelling academically, she learned numerous languages (e.g., French, English, German, and Finnish, besides her native Russian) and received the best education possible. She became interested in the socialist ideas in the atmosphere at the time, initially helping in the local library and spreading literacy among workers.

After returning from Switzerland where she studied economics, Alexandra became a devout Marxist and joined the Russian Social Democratic Labour Party, eventually siding with the Mensheviks after they split from Bolsheviks, in 1906. She toured Europe, meeting fellow Marxists and women's rights activist.

Returning to Russia in 1917, she sided with Lenin. She was instrumental in the formation of Zhenotdel, a women's department of the Communist Party. After centuries of a rigid patriarchal atmosphere in Russia, Alexandra tried to improve the condition of women, who were often the ones suffering the most under the burden of the imperial regime and later under the Communists.

Due to her constant opposition to some of the policies proposed by Lenin, most importantly his NEP, Alexandra was quickly sidelined and almost expulsed from the party. Realizing that there was no place for her in the USSR, Alexandra demanded to be placed as an ambassador, and Stalin promptly granted this request. From then on, Alexandra traveled across the globe, from Norway, to Mexico, again to Norway, and finally to Sweden. She returned to Moscow shortly before her death in 1952.

Alexandra Kollontai around 1900.
https://commons.wikimedia.org/w/index.php?curid=88240669

Conclusion

It is very easy (and indeed most people feel obliged) to abhor the sheer amount of violence bred by the Communist revolution in Russia. The Communists committed numerous crimes, executed millions of innocent people, and made life miserable for many more millions.

Instead of bringing an age of freedom and prosperity after centuries of tsarist autocracy, the Communists only tightened the grip, making all peoples of the USSR suffer greatly. However, the world we live in today is very much shaped by the USSR, including its darkest period of Stalinism. We simply don't know how the world would look had it not been for this Communist behemoth, this gigantic country that somehow managed to endure everything—and not simply endure but propel humanity into new phases of development. First, we must not forget that the USSR was instrumental in defeating what's arguably an even worse Nazi regime. We mustn't forget that the Soviets developed their first nuclear bomb in 1949 (though probably aided by Soviet spies within the Manhattan Project). By 1961, they tested the most powerful weapon known to mankind: the "Tsar bomb," an advanced thermonuclear bomb.

In 1961, another important breakthrough was made. Namely, Yuri Gagarin reached outer space in *Vostok 1*. The Soviets were a force to be reckoned with, and they provided at least some kind of balance to a world increasingly dominated by the United States. The precarious geopolitical balance of the Cold War era was at least some kind of balance, and despite all the crises, we're alive today to talk about it.

What would have happened if the Whites prevailed? Would they be able to stop the Nazi tide? The Nazis needed vast Soviet lands and resources to fuel their grand, inhumane plans. As far as we know, only the Soviets with their strict and ruthless discipline could stop the Nazis. (Weakened by their eastward offensive, the Nazis soon lost their foothold in France and Italy.) Had the Whites prevailed, the outcome may have been similar to WWI's or, even worse, a total defeat.

The USSR, we must also emphasize, was the first Communist state in the world. All the other Communist countries, such as China, were decidedly inspired (and often aided) by the USSR. And while the USSR ceased to exist, China is slowly taking the role of USSR as the country that provides a counter-balancing force to the West.

Fast forwarding to 1989 and the fall of the Berlin Wall, we come to the end of the Soviet dream. Though helping spread Communism all around the world (e.g., Romania, Bulgaria, China, Vietnam, North Korea, Congo, Ethiopia, South Africa, Chile, Peru, Argentina, Brazil, etc.), the USSR ceased to exist and quite literally crumbled under its own weight in what is deemed by some to be the "greatest geopolitical tragedy of the 20th century." But its mark will continue to pervade global politics and geopolitical balance in the years to come, leaving us with mere conjectures and shaky suppositions about what would have happened had the USSR never came into being.

Here's another book by Enthralling History that you might like

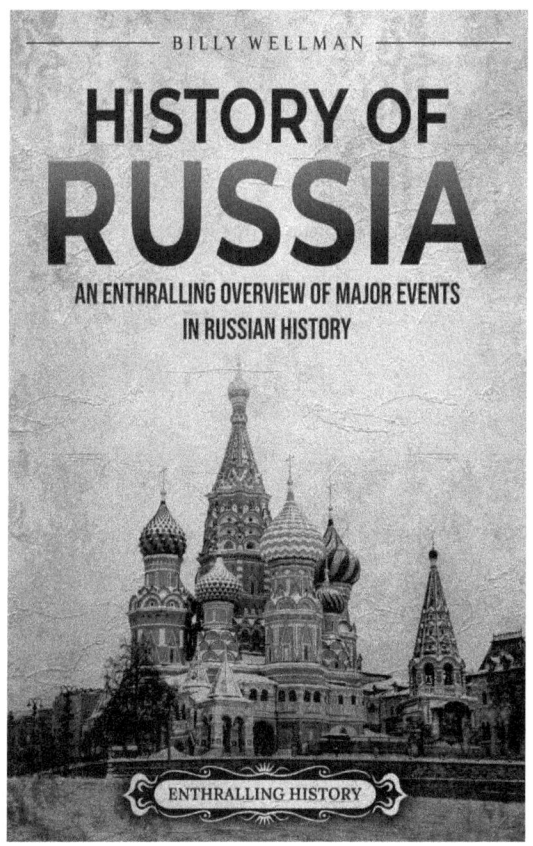

Free limited time bonus

Stop for a moment. We have a free bonus set up for you. The problem is this: we forget 90% of everything that we read after 7 days. Crazy fact, right? Here's the solution: we've created a printable, 1-page pdf summary for this book that you're reading now. All you have to do to get your free pdf summary is to go to the following website:

https://livetolearn.lpages.co/enthrallinghistory/

Once you do, it will be intuitive. Enjoy, and thank you!

Bibliography

PERRIE, Maureen; LIEVEN, Dominic CB; SUNY, Ronald Grigor (ed.). *The Cambridge History of Russia: Volume 1, From Early Rus' to 1689*. Cambridge University Press, 2006.

KORPELA, Jukka. *Prince, Saint, and Apostle: Prince Vladimir Svjatoslavič of Kiev, His Posthumous Life, and the Religious Legitimization of the Russian Great Power*. Otto Harrassowitz Verlag, 2001.

NESTOR, *Laurentian Text*. p. 112. Available at: https://www.mgh-bibliothek.de/dokumente/a/a011458.pdf

DE MADARIAGA, Isabel. *Ivan the Terrible*. Yale University Press, 2006.

ANISIMOV, Evgeniĭ Viktorovich. *The reforms of Peter the Great: progress through coercion in Russia*. ME Sharpe, 1993.

DE MADARIAGA, Isabel. *Catherine the Great*. Macmillan Education UK, 1990.

KIIANSKAIA, O. I. Decembrists in Russian History and Historiography: Polemical Notes. *Rossiia i sovremennyi mir*, 2017, 2: 95.

O'MEARA, Patrick. *The Decembrist Pavel Pestel: Russia's First Republican*. Springer, 2016.

TROYAN, N. The Philosophical Opinions of the Petrashevsky Circle. *Philosophy and Phenomenological Research*, 1946, 6.3: 363-380.

KARAKASIS, Georgios, et al. The Catechism of Destruction: Sergei Nechaev and the spirit of Nihilism. *ICOANA CREDINTEI. International Journal of Interdisciplinary Scientific Research*, 2018, 4.08: 103-114.

BAKUNIN, Mikhail Aleksandrovich. *God and the State*. Courier Corporation, 1970.

NICHOLAS, I. (2014). ALEXANDER II OF RUSSIA (1818-1881). *Famous Assassinations in World History: An Encyclopedia [2 volumes]*, 12.

POMPER, Philip. *Lenin's brother: the origins of the October Revolution*. WW Norton & Company, 2010.

FERRO, Marc. *Nicholas II: Last of the Tsars*. Oxford University Press on Demand, 1995.

KING, Greg. *The Last Empress: The Life and Times of Alexandra Feodorovna, Tsarina of Russia*. Birch Lane Press, 1994.

KOWNER, Rotem. Nicholas II and the Japanese body: Images and decision-making on the eve of the Russo-Japanese War. *The Psychohistory Review*, 1998, 26.3: 211.

LOWE, Charles. *Alexander III of Russia*. London: W. Heinemann, 1895.

KING, Greg; ASHTON, Janet. 'A Programme for the Reign': Press, Propaganda and Public Opinion at Russia's Last Coronation. *Electronic British Library Journal*, 2012, 1-27.

KOTSONIS, Yanni. The problem of the individual in the Stolypin reforms. *Kritika: Explorations in Russian and Eurasian History*, 2011, 12.1: 25-52.

WILSON, Sandra. *The Russo-Japanese War and Japan: politics, nationalism and historical memory*. Palgrave Macmillan UK, 1999.

KOWNER, Rotem (ed.). *The impact of the Russo-Japanese war*. London: Routledge, 2007.

ANISIN, Alexei. The Russian Bloody Sunday Massacre of 1905: a discursive account of nonviolent transformation. *Politics, Groups, and Identities*, 2014, 2.4: 643-660.

HARIHARAN, Krishnan. Eisenstein and the Potemkin Revolution. *Social Scientist*, 1979, 54-61.

DULEBOHN, Jeanne Louise. *The Bulygin Duma, February-September, 1905: A Study in the History of the Russian Revolution*. University of Minnesota, 1949.

MCKEAN, Robert B. The Constitutional Monarchy in Russia, 1906-17. In: *Regime and Society in Twentieth-Century Russia: Selected Papers from the Fifth World Congress of Central and East European Studies, Warsaw, 1995*. Palgrave Macmillan UK, 1999. p. 44-67.

HASEGAWA, Tsuyoshi. Lenin: A Biography. *Journal of Interdisciplinary History*, 2003, 33.3: 482-484.

YEDLIN, Tova. *Maxim Gorky: A political biography*. Greenwood Publishing Group, 1999. Available at: http://www.arvindguptatoys.com/arvindgupta/rus-gorky-biography.pdf

CARR, E. H.; CARR, E. H. Bolsheviks and Mensheviks. *The Bolshevik Revolution 1917-1923: Volume One*, 1950, 26-44.

PHILLIPS, Steve. *Lenin and the Russian Revolution*. Heinemann, 2000. P. 27.

BECHERELLI, Alberto; BIAGINI, Antenllo; MOTTA, Giovanna. Remembering Gavrilo Princip. *The First World War: Analysis and Interpretation*, 2015, 1: 17-33.

MELANCON, Michael. Rethinking Russia's February Revolution: anonymous spontaneity or socialist agency? *The Carl Beck Papers in Russian and East European Studies*, 2000, 1408: 48.; p. 6.

SCHAPIRO, Leonard. The Political Thought of the First Provisional Government. In: *Revolutionary Russia*. Harvard University Press, 1968. p. 97-113.

HASEGAWA, T. (1977). The Bolsheviks and the formation of the Petrograd soviet in the February Revolution. *Soviet Studies*, 29(1), 86-107.

LENIN, Vladimir. *Lenin Collected Works*, Progress Publishers, 1964, Moscow, Volume 24

LENIN, Vladimir. *The Development of Capitalism in Russia*, Marxist Archivepp. 37-38.

MARX, Karl, *Das Kapital*, II, 303.

LENIN, Vladimir, *Materialism and Empirio-criticism*. Marxist Archive.

RABINOWITCH, Alexander. *Prelude to revolution: The Petrograd Bolsheviks and the July 1917 uprising*. Indiana University Press, 1991.

ASCHER, Abraham. The Kornilov Affair. *Russian Review*, 1953, 12.4: 235-252.

CARR, Edward Hallett. *The Bolshevik Revolution, 1917-1923*. WW Norton & Company, 1985.

CHANNON, John. The Bolsheviks and the peasantry: The land question during the first eight months of Soviet rule. *The Slavonic and East European Review*, 1988, 66.4: 593-624.

HERLIHY, Patricia. The Russian Vodka Prohibition of 1914 and Its Consequences. *Dual Markets: Comparative Approaches to Regulation*, 2017, 193-206.

MELGUNOFF, Sergei. The Record of the Red Terror. *Current History (1916-1940)*, 1927, 27.2: 198-205.

MALLE, Silvana. *The economic organization of War Communism 1918-1921*. Cambridge University Press, 2002.

WILLIAMS, Christopher. The 1921 Russian famine: Centre and periphery responses. *Revolutionary Russia*, 1993, 6.2: 277-314.

LAUCHLAN, Iain. Guardians of the People's Total Happiness: The Origins and Impact of the Cult of the Cheka. *Politics, Religion & Ideology*, 2013, 14.4:

522-540.

MARTIN, Latsis, *Red Terror*, no 1, Kazan, 1 November 1918, p. 2.

LENIN, V. I. Collected Works. SPEECH AT A RALLY AND CONCERT FOR THE ALL-RUSSIA EXTRAORDINARY COMMISSION STAFF NOVEMBER 7, 1918. Available at: https://www.marxists.org/archive/lenin/works/cw/pdf/lenin-cw-vol-28.pdf

SCHNEER, Jonathan. *The Lockhart Plot: Love, Betrayal, Assassination and Counter-Revolution in Lenin's Russia*. Oxford University Press, USA, 2020.

SMITH, Scott B. Who Shot Lenin? Fania Kaplan, the SR Underground, and the August 1918 Assassination Attempt on Lenin. *Jahrbücher für Geschichte Osteuropas*, 1998, H. 1: 100-119.

ERICH SENN, Alfred; GOLDBERG, Harold J. The Assassination of Count Mirbach. *Canadian Slavonic Papers*, 1979, 21.4: 438-445.

HAFNER, Lutz. The Assassination of Count Mirbach and the "July Uprising" of the Left Socialist Revolutionaries in Moscow, 1918. *The Russian Review*, 1991, 50.3: 324-344.

SINGLETON, Seth. The Tambov Revolt (1920-1921). *Slavic Review*, 1966, 25.3: 497-512.

ERICKSON, John. The Origins of the Red Army. In: *Revolutionary Russia*. Harvard University Press, 1968. p. 224-258.

TROTSKY, Leon. My life. Available at: https://www.marxists.org/archive/trotsky/1930/mylife/ch34.htm

BORTNEVSKI, Viktor G. White Administration and White Terror (the Denikin Period). *The Russian Review*, 1993, 52.3: 354-366.

HUGHES, Matthew, et al. Allied Intervention in the Russian Civil War. *The Palgrave Concise Historical Atlas of the First World War*, 2005, 98-99.

BUDNITSKII, Oleg. Jews, pogroms, and the White movement: a historiographical critique. *Kritika: Explorations in Russian and Eurasian History*, 2001, 2.4: 1-23.

LEHOVICH, Dimitry V. Denikin's Offensive. *The Russian Review*, 1973, 32.2: 173-186.

PETERS, Victor. *Nestor Makhno*. Winnipeg: Echo Books, 1971. Available at: https://files.libcom.org/files/Victor_Peters_Makhno.pdf

MALET, Michael; The End, October 1920–August 1921. *Nestor Makhno in the Russian Civil War*, 1982, 64-80.

GILLEY, Christopher. Fighters for Ukrainian independence? Imposture and identity among Ukrainian warlords, 1917–22. *Historical Research*, 2017, 90.247: 172-190.

DARCH, Colin, 2020, Nestor Makhno and Rural Anarchism in Ukraine. *Pluto Press*. Available at: https://diasporiana.org.ua/wp-content/uploads/books/26581/file.pdf

WEISSMAN, Benjamin M. *Herbert Hoover and Famine Relief to Soviet Russia, 1921-1923*. Hoover Institution Press, 1974.

POLLACK, Emanuel. *The Kronstadt Rebellion: The First Armed Revolt Against the Soviets*. Philosophical Library, 1959.

RICHMAN, Sheldon L. War Communism to NEP: the road from serfdom. *The Journal of Libertarian Studies*, 1981, 5.1: 89-97.

PICKERSGILL, Joyce E. Hyperinflation and Monetary Reform in the Soviet Union, 1921-26. *Journal of Political Economy*, 1968, 76.5: 1037-1048.

EFREMOV, Steven M. *The role of inflation in soviet history: Prices, living standards, and political change*. 2012. PhD Thesis. East Tennessee State University.

SOKOLOV, N. G. The Use of Barter During the Transition to NEP. *Soviet Studies in History*, 1984, 23.2: 54-61.

EFREMOV, Steven M. *The role of inflation in soviet history: Prices, living standards, and political change*. 2012. PhD Thesis. East Tennessee State University.

BARNETT, Vincent. As Good as Gold? A Note on the chervonets. *Europe-Asia Studies*, 1994, 46.4: 663-669.

BALL, Alan M. *Russia's last capitalists: the Nepmen, 1921-1929*. Univ of California Press, 1990.

CORBESERO, Susan. History, Myth, and Memory: A Biography of a Stalin Portrait. *Russian History*, 2011, 38.1: 58-84.

READ, Christopher. *Stalin: From the Caucasus to the Kremlin*. Taylor & Francis, 2016.

STALIN, Joseph. *Marxism and the National Question*. Internet Archive; p. 16.

BROWN, Archie. The Power of the General Secretary of the CPSU. *Authority, power and policy in the USSR: Essays Dedicated to Leonard Schapiro*, 1983, 135-157.

LENIN, Vladimir Ilich Ulyanov. Letters to the Congress. Available at: https://www.marxists.org/archive/lenin/works/1922/dec/testamnt/congress.htm

O'CONNOR, Timothy Edward. *Stalin and Trotsky 1926-1928*. PhD Thesis. Graduate School. P. 24

KNICKERBOCKER, H. R. The Soviet Five-Year Plan. *International Affairs (Royal Institute of International Affairs 1931-1939)*, 1931, 10.4: 433-459. P. 434.

ANFERTIEV, Ivan A. LD Trotsky, GE Zinoviev, and LB Kamenev: the Failed Successors to VI Lenin. *RSUH/RGGU Bulletin: "Literary Theory. Linguistics. Cultural Studies," Series*, 2018, 5: 37-48.

HUTLEY, F. C. The Moscow Trials. *The Australian Quarterly*, 1937, 9.2: 77-86.

GESEEN, Keith. How Stalin Became Stalinist. *The New Yorker.* 2017. https://www.newyorker.com/magazine/2017/11/06/how-stalin-became-stalinist

STALIN, J.V. Y.M. Sverdlov. Available at: https://www.marxists.org/reference/archive/stalin/works/1924/11/x01.htm

www.ingramcontent.com/pod-product-compliance
Lightning Source LLC
Chambersburg PA
CBHW070338010526
44107CB00004B/541